. . . .

MAKING PEACE WORK:
THE ROLE OF THE
INTERNATIONAL DEVELOPMENT
COMMUNITY

POLICY ESSAY NO.18
· · · · · · · · · · · · · · · · · · · ·

MAKING PEACE WORK:

THE ROLE OF THE INTERNATIONAL DEVELOPMENT COMMUNITY

NICOLE BALL WITH TAMMY HALEVY

DISTRIBUTED BY THE JOHNS HOPKINS UNIVERSITY PRESS
PUBLISHED BY THE OVERSEAS DEVELOPMENT COUNCIL
WASHINGTON, DC

Copyright © 1996 by Overseas Development Council, Washington, DC

Distributed by:
The Johns Hopkins University Press
2715 North Charles Street
Baltimore, MD 21218-431

Library of Congress Cataloging-In-Publication Data

Ball, Nicole
  Making peace work: the role of the international development community/Nicole Ball with Tammy Halevy

Policy Essay No. 18
Includes bibliographic references.
  1. Economic assistance. 2. Peace. I. Halevy, Tammy. II. Title.

HC60.B26858   1996   338.9′1—dc20   96-33786 CIP

ISBN: 1-56517-022-9

Printed in the United States of America.

Director of Publications: Christine E. Contee
Publications Editor: Jacqueline Edlund-Braun
Edited by Elizabeth Reed Forsyth
Cover design: Ripe Studios

Contents

Foreword

In the last half of this century the world has seen people, nations, and economies ravaged by war; as the authors of this study point out, some 45 million people have perished and additional tens of millions of people have been displaced due to conflicts throughout the world. But with the end of the Cold War have come efforts to halt wars, and the international community is increasingly being called on to help sustain and consolidate the peace.

This is a relatively new endeavor for the development cooperation agencies, but the 1990s have provided a valuable experience base in strategies for addressing the needs of post-conflict countries. ODC's Program on Enhancing Security and Development examined the experiences of the peace processes in Cambodia, El Salvador, Mozambique, and Nicaragua. Experts from the regions and the United States sought to identify a donors' action agenda in support of post-conflict reconstruction, political reconciliation, and renewed development in the countries under study. Using the case studies as the basis for a broader discussion of the issues, the authors of this volume derive lessons for peacebuilding with a focus on the role of the international community, particularly the development assistance agencies.

The program was directed by ODC Fellow Nicole Ball, an expert on security and development issues. Her earlier ODC Policy Essay, *Pressing for Peace*, considered the potential for using economic incentives to encourage and support changes in the military sector of recipient countries.

The Policy Essay series, now in its sixth year, provides a forum for authors to express opinions, make predictions, and assess policy ramifications of development topics of international concern. The relatively abbreviated format is short enough to serve as a digestible brief for policymaking, yet lengthy enough to allow room for more extended analysis.

The Overseas Development Council gratefully acknowledges The Asia Foundation, The Ford Foundation/Office for Mexico and Central America, The Netherlands Ministry of Foreign Affairs, The Swedish International Development Agency, Swiss Development Cooperation, and The Winston Foundation for World Peace for their support of the Program on Enhancing Security and Development. We owe a particular expression of thanks to Lawrence Condon, Robert Crane, Priscilla Hayner, and The Joyce Mertz-Gilmore Foundation, whose early enthusiasm and support were crucial to getting this project off the ground. ODC also wishes to acknowledge the generous support of The Ford Foundation and The Rockefeller Foundation for the Council's overall program.

John W. Sewell
President
March 1996

Acknowledgments

Many individuals in the policy and research communities have generously shared their knowledge and assessments of post-conflict peace-building efforts, and the authors wish to thank them for their willingness both to give us the benefit of their experiences and insights and to answer innumerable questions.

We particularly wish to express our appreciation for the contributions of the researchers who have been affiliated with this project: Miguel de Brito, Frederick Brown, Margarita Castillo, Melba Castillo, Rafael Guido Bejar, João Honwana, Nelly Miranda, Robert Muscat, Herman Rosa Chavez, Elisa dos Santos, and Alexander Segovia. From them we have learned much about the complexities of war-to-peace transformations.

The project also benefited from the advice of an international advisory panel: Antonia Chayes, Michael Chege, Paul Collier, Jorge Dominguez, Xabier Gorostiaga, S.J., David Hamburg, Reverend J. Bryan Hehir, Jonathan Moore, Carin Norberg, Ambassador Olara Otunnu, Ambassador Alvaro de Soto, Julia Taft, and Michael Ward.

In addition, this manuscript has been thoughtfully reviewed by a number of practitioners and policy analysts whose comments and suggestions have greatly improved its quality: Mats Bernal, James Boyce, Andrew Carl, Christine Contee, Antonio Donini, Iain Guest, Catherine Gwin, Elizabeth Uphoff Kato, Krishna Kumar, Aileen Marshall, Steve Morrison, Marina Ottaway, Matthias Stiefel, Necla Tschirgi, George Vickers, and Patricia Weiss Fagen.

Executive Summary

In the first 50 years following World War II, some 45 million people perished as a result of armed conflict. Many of these conflicts were of long duration and profoundly disrupted the economic, social, and institutional fabric of the countries and regions in which they occurred. The magnitude of damage to infrastructure, depletion of human resources, militarization, lack of government legitimacy, societal trauma, and institutional weaknesses distinguishes war-torn societies from countries undergoing economic or political transitions under more peaceful conditions. The effects of war-induced isolation on individuals and geographic regions, the influence of peace treaties on the scope and pace of change, and the extent and urgency of the problems place additional burdens on war-torn societies.

The international community has come to recognize that warring parties require assistance not only in negotiating peace agreements but also in sustaining and consolidating the peace. *Making Peace Work* extracts lessons for future peacebuilding efforts from the recent experiences of Cambodia, El Salvador, Mozambique, and Nicaragua as they have sought to rebuild their political and economic systems and repair their social fabric. Many of these lessons offer guidance to the international community in general as well as to the governments and citizens of war-torn societies. This essay focuses primarily on the implications of these lessons for development cooperation agencies.

DONOR SUPPORT FOR THE PEACE PROCESS

■   THE SUPPORT THAT VARIOUS MEMBERS of the international community can provide to the peace process varies both by institution and phase of the peace process. In the countries that form the core of this study, civil wars ended with negotiated settlements—that is, without a clear victor—and the peace process had four phases: negotiation, cessation of hostilities, transition, and consolidation. When one party triumphs, the phases of the peace process are not as clear-cut, but the problems that must be overcome are similar.

During *negotiations*, the main objective is to reach a political agreement on key issues so that fighting can stop. The donors need to devote only a relatively modest amount of resources at this point. They should focus on planning for post-conflict rebuilding and on developing collaborative relationships with the parties to the conflict as well as with civil society. Donors can also provide mediators and the parties with advice on issues under negotiation in their areas of institutional expertise.

During the *cessation of hostilities* phase, donors can begin to match assumptions made during planning with realities on the ground. They can also provide assistance for activities that will begin once the peace agreement has been signed, such as equipping assembly areas for troops to be demobilized or clearing mines from critical areas. The cessation of hostilities phase is normally brief, but it may be extended as a result of political jockeying; if this occurs, it may be desirable and possible to undertake other activities, such as assisting the repatriation of refugees and the repair of critical infrastructure. Although such activities may encourage the parties to resolve their differences, the possibility always exists that the peace process will break down and hostilities will resume. Donors are, therefore, typically cautious about what can be accomplished during this period.

The *transition phase* begins once hostilities have been formally concluded and generally lasts until a multiparty election has been held. The major objectives of the transition phase are to establish a government with sufficient domestic and international legitimacy to operate effectively and to assist the parties to comply with the terms of the peace accords. However, peace accords vary considerably in their comprehensiveness. Some cover only a small portion of the many activities required to strengthen the institutional base of war-torn countries, consolidate internal and external security, and promote economic and social revitalization. It is thus important that the international community assist the parties to prioritize the tasks of peacebuilding.

This phase of the peace process places the heaviest demand on the international community for diplomatic, financial, military, and technical assistance. Various institutions offer the financial and technical resources required during the transition phase: international donors, including multilateral development banks and U.N. agencies; foreign, defense, and justice ministries; nongovernmental and private international organizations; and the private sector.

Due to the differences among countries, it is difficult to develop a generic list of priorities for peacebuilding activities. However, the experiences of recent peace processes suggest that the following activities should receive early attention even when they are not specified in the peace accords:

- Provide a sufficient level of internal security to enable economic activity to recover, to encourage refugees and internally displaced persons to reestablish themselves, and to persuade the business community to invest;
- Strengthen government's capacity to carry out key activities;
- Assist the return of refugees and internally displaced persons;
- Support the rejuvenation of household economies, especially by strengthening the smallholder agricultural sector through the provision of inputs such as basic tools, seeds, and draft animals;
- Assist the recovery of communities, in part through projects that rehabilitate social and economic infrastructure;
- Rehabilitate economic infrastructure of crucial importance for economic revival, such as major roads, bridges, marketplaces, and power generation facilities;
- Remove land mines from major transport arteries, fields in heavily populated areas, and other critical sites;
- Stabilize the national currency and rehabilitate financial institutions;
- Promote national reconciliation; and
- Give priority to the basic needs of social groups and geographic areas most affected by the conflict.

With the installation of a government selected in a multiparty election, a country moves into the *consolidation phase*. The major objective of this phase is to continue implementing the peace accords, because some reforms mandated by peace agreements may take longer to execute than the one to two years that the transition phase typically lasts. In addition, although the provisions of the peace accords may constitute necessary steps toward consolidating peace, they rarely deal adequately with the problems that led to the war or create an environment conducive to resolving future conflicts peacefully. Therefore, the reform process must be deepened during the consolidation phase so that issues such as significant economic imbalances among social groups and the lack of mechanisms to prevent human-rights abuses can be addressed, even if they are not enshrined in the peace agreements.

. . . .

LESSONS LEARNED

■ THE DEVELOPMENT COOPERATION AGENCIES have gained valuable experience since the beginning of the 1990s in addressing the needs of post-conflict countries. Six key lessons about the scope and delivery of this assistance have emerged from ODC's examination of recent peacebuilding efforts.

■ *Constraints on the scope, design, and delivery of relief and long-term development assistance make necessary a new form of aid for the transition phase of the peace process: post-conflict transition assistance.* Meeting the objectives of peacebuilding requires supporting activities not traditionally within the purview of either relief or development assistance. It also places a premium on financial flexibility, contingency planning, sensitivity to local conditions, and conflict resolution techniques and objectives. What is more, the benchmarks used to measure progress may need to be qualitatively different from those applied to development programs, and the performance targets may need to be less demanding than those applied to countries that have not experienced prolonged civil wars.

■ *The international donor community has an important role to play during all four phases of the peace process.* Donors should be involved from the negotiation through the consolidation phase.

To maximize their input during the negotiation phase, donors should establish technical advisory committees to ensure that economic considerations are discussed during negotiations and to clarify the nature and amount of external assistance that will be forthcoming. They should also explore the opportunities for creating working groups before the accords are signed to foster the development of good relations among donors, the parties to the conflict, and other societal groups. All of these activities would encourage donors to undertake advance planning.

During the consolidation phase, donors should collaborate with other members of the international community to ensure that key reforms remain high on the agenda of the new government and to provide war-torn societies with assistance to meet these objectives.

■ *A fundamental reform of the security sector is critical to the ultimate consolidation of peace.* In collaboration with other members of the international community, donors should vigorously promote reform of the security sector during all phases of the peace process. In particular, they should provide assistance to develop good budgeting practices in the security sector, expand the pool of civilian security analysts, and civilianize the police forces. In addition, they should encourage civilian-military dialogue and civilian control of all security forces. Donors should make maximum use of consultative groups and roundtables to ensure that these issues are on the government's agenda.

■ *Program selection, design, and implementation cannot be approached from a purely technical perspective or without consideration of the political situation.* Peacebuilding activities are inherently political and are implemented in highly politicized environments. Political considerations can both improve and detract from program quality, and donors need to minimize the negative effects and maximize the positive ones.

As a first step, donors should analyze how the post-conflict political environment will affect their operations. Their staff should incorporate the political dimension into their analyses and bear in mind political obstacles to the programs they develop. Donors also need to be alert to the fact that political considerations often drive the parties' choice about the content of peacebuilding programs in ways that foreclose theoretically desirable options and impede the implementation of programs.

■ *Donors urgently need to consider how external assistance can best be used to strengthen the government's capacity to perform key tasks during the transition phase without bolstering its capacity to use resources for partisan political purposes.* Restarting government has rarely received the attention it deserves given the extreme weakness of the public sector in countries emerging from prolonged internal conflicts.

Toward this end, donors might establish a donor-government forum that would serve three purposes: 1) foster the development of a policy framework for peacebuilding activities; 2) identify the key tasks for government, a priority ranking of tasks, and the appropriate level of government to assume responsibility for each task; and 3) promote national reconciliation by incorporating input from both the former armed opposition and from civil society into the deliberations of this forum.

A second mechanism to strengthen government capacity would be a local committee composed of government representatives, community leaders, local nongovernmental organizations, members of the business community, and other citizens. This committee would provide input on a range of issues pertaining to the design and implementation of peacebuilding projects or programs. In addition to building capacity, these committees could promote national reconciliation and improve the design and execution of programs.

■ *Coordination is vital to capitalize on the fairly short window of opportunity for fundamental political and economic restructuring that generally follows civil wars.* Aid coordination is notoriously difficult to achieve, and in post-conflict environments, both the need and the constraints are magnified.

Due to the quantity and urgency of the demands on all actors, the most critical period for donor coordination is the transition phase. So far, the mechanisms for coordinating donor activities have suffered from shortcomings such as inadequate involvement of the local donor community, unclear lines of authority, and poorly coordinated hand-off of ongoing programs at the conclusion of the peacekeeping operation.

One means of avoiding these problems might be to appoint the U.N. resident coordinator as the deputy head of the peacekeeping operation for peacebuilding activities, supported by a coordinating committee composed of members of the resident donor community. Absent a U.N. resident coordinator, the World Bank resident representative or a senior bilateral donor representative could assume this responsibility. To function efficiently, this mechanism would need the strong and consistent support at the highest level of all relevant institutions.

Finally, the efficient use of external resources requires not only that donors coordinate their activities, but also that host governments coordinate the inflow of external financing to avoid unnecessary duplication and to mesh donor activities with government priorities. This requires donors to provide host governments with detailed information about the nature and extent of their financial assistance. If sufficient capacity exists, it may be desirable to develop a central aid coordination unit, but such a unit should not usurp the functions of line ministries.

. . . .

PRIORITY TASKS FOR DONORS

■ THE LESSONS LEARNED from recent peacebuilding efforts demonstrate that donors and other members of the international community could improve the effectiveness of their assistance in a number of ways. Two areas should be priorities for donors: 1) issues that can be addressed immediately, and 2) areas where gaps in current understanding argue strongly in favor of further analysis.

IMMEDIATE ACTIONS

■ The senior managers of donor agencies should transmit two messages to their staff. First, an immediate return to traditional development activities is neither possible nor desirable in post-conflict environments. Second, peacebuilding is not a distraction from development efforts, but a critical precondition for development following conflicts. In consequence, priority must be given to addressing the three broad objectives of peacebuilding: strengthening political institutions, enhancing internal and external security, and promoting economic and social revitalization.

■ Donors should take steps to lengthen the time frame for post-conflict peacebuilding activities. The current planning cycle of two to three years is insufficient to foster the adoption of policies and patterns of behavior that will minimize disparities among social groups and maximize the opportunities for resolving disputes peacefully. Current planning practices and guidelines should be reviewed to eliminate, where possible, impediments to adopting a longer time frame.

■ To maximize the effectiveness of the external resources invested in peacebuilding, a division of labor urgently needs to be established between donors and other members of the international community and among bilateral and multilateral development cooperation agencies. Institutional turf battles, which prevail over collaboration in many instances, undermine the effectiveness of resources invested in peacebuilding and damage the long-term prospects of war-torn societies. Mechanisms should be developed to reinforce the preferences for institutional collaboration, and senior managers should consistently and forcefully deliver the message that collaboration is the order of the day.

■ To improve the efficiency and quality of their support for peacebuilding efforts, donors should: 1) develop cooperative relations with the parties to the conflict as early in the peace process as possible to enable meaningful planning to begin before the peace accords have been signed; 2) enhance the flexibility of their funding; 3) ensure that personnel are carefully matched to the jobs to which they are assigned; 4) evaluate political obstacles as part of program design; and 5) require greater accountability from implementing agencies. Most of these changes require time to implement fully, but the groundwork should be laid as soon as possible.

■ Donors should use informal policy dialogue and formal performance criteria to press for full compliance with the terms of the peace agreements. This pressure should be exerted, however, in a manner consistent with the peace accords rather than to the partisan advantage of the donors themselves.

■ Donors should make every effort to ensure that peacebuilding activities enhance national reconciliation. Two key objectives in this regard are to create: 1) conditions in which the parties to the conflict focus on solving specific problems, rather than using peacebuilding programs to continue their efforts to dominate one another; and 2) opportunities for participation by civil society.

■ In view of the institutional weakness of post-conflict societies, donors need to give top priority to building capacity in both the public sector and civil society as early as possible. In the public sector, the objectives should be to identify key tasks of government, to prioritize those tasks according to both time and appropriate implementing agency, and to determine the assistance needed to increase the capacity of government to carry out these tasks independently and in an apolitical manner. In civil society, the objectives should be to enhance the capacity of organizations to evaluate policy and to develop and implement programs in their sphere of activity.

ISSUES FOR FURTHER CONSIDERATION

■ The current transition phase, which normally lasts between one and two years, is too short, and holding elections so soon after the termination of hostilities tends to close the reform process prematurely. It would be useful to examine how long and under what conditions the transition phase could be extended and how the country would be governed during this longer transition period.

■ Donors are confronted with the simultaneous need to develop new policies for post-conflict environments and to implement peacebuilding programs. The force of events will require that many changes be made before adequate reflection can take place. Nonetheless, analytic work should continue in order to gain a deeper understanding of the internal dynamics of donor assistance for peacebuilding. It would be helpful for donors to examine their own policies and activities and for external analysts to conduct case studies of specific donors in the same way that they have evaluated peacebuilding activities in particular war-torn countries.

■ In-depth analyses of specific types of peacebuilding activities could be helpful in determining the most cost-effective method of meeting specific objectives. Virtually every donor institution is facing financial constraints, and these are likely to intensify in the near term. It is critical that donors evaluate just what their financial investment buys.

■ ■ ■

Post-conflict reconstruction has now captured the attention of the international development community. As this essay demonstrates, there is sufficient accumulated experience from past peacebuilding efforts to identify the broad outlines of a donor strategy for post-conflict reconstruction and reconciliation. The next step is to agree on priority areas and translate this experience into operational guidelines for each of those areas. At the same time, the international community should not lose sight of the fact that the responsibility for moving from war to peace is ultimately the responsibility of the people and the governments of war-torn countries. Donor strategies need, therefore, to give particular emphasis to creating an environment in which reconstruction and reconciliation can take root and to building capacity in both the public and the private sectors. Only then will war-torn countries be able to take advantage of a climate favorable to the consolidation of peace.

Part I
Introduction

....
REBUILDING WAR-TORN SOCIETIES

■ CONFLICT HAS COST THE LIVES of some 45 million people over the last 50 years. In 1994 alone, an estimated 43 million persons were displaced throughout the world, most forced from their homes by armed conflict. Although civil strife remains a central characteristic of the post-Cold War era, efforts to halt wars have achieved partial success in Angola, Bosnia-Herzegovina, Cambodia, El Salvador, Ethiopia/Eritrea, Haiti, Mozambique, Namibia, and Nicaragua, as well as in West Bank/Gaza.

Most of these conflicts were of long duration and profoundly disrupted the economic, social, and institutional fabric of the countries and regions in which they occurred. Millions of people were killed, injured, or forced into exile as civilians became the explicit target of warfare. Societies were traumatized as wars turned family members, friends, and neighbors into enemies. Economies, which were in most cases fragile to begin with, were unable to provide many basic goods and services by war's end, and political structures frequently needed to be built from the ground up. The proliferation of weapons and the militarization of relations between citizens and the state seriously complicated the efforts to resolve these problems.

At the end of such wars, peace agreements engender enormous expectations. The signing of the peace agreement and achievement of a cease-fire may be seen as signals that all outstanding issues have been resolved and that compliance with the accords will complete the peace process. A corollary to this is the belief that the reforms envisioned by the accords can be implemented within a year or, at most, two years under the auspices of a peacekeeping operation and that the agreement provides a detailed road map for consolidating the peace.

Unfortunately, these expectations are almost uniformly misplaced. For agreements to be acceptable to all parties, many issues either cannot be dealt with at all or can be addressed only superficially. At best, peace agreements provide a framework for ending hostilities and a guide to handling the initial stages of post-conflict reform. After the agreement is signed, discussions often must be held about how the provisions should be implemented and about how critical issues not covered in the agreement should be addressed.

Furthermore, implementing even the limited reforms called for in peace agreements often takes more than a year or two. Given the range of problems that need to be addressed and the length of time required to achieve rehabilitation, reconstruction, and reconciliation, it is not unreasonable to expect that the international community will have to remain involved for perhaps ten years following signature of the accords. The nature and intensity of this involvement will vary over time.

To succeed, peace processes need the sustained involvement of the range of institutions that constitute the international community (see Box 1), and each external actor has a specific role to play in the peace

BOX 1. KEY DEFINITIONS

INTERNATIONAL COMMUNITY. The international community consists of bilateral government agencies such as ministries of foreign affairs, defense, and justice; multilateral political institutions such as the United Nations; regional organizations such as the Organization of African Unity and the North Atlantic Treaty Organization; members of the international development community; international religious organizations; international human rights organizations; and international political parties.

INTERNATIONAL DEVELOPMENT COMMUNITY. The international development community consists of bilateral and multilateral development assistance agencies such as the U.S. Agency for International Development and the U.N. Development Programme (UNDP), the international financial institutions such as the International Monetary Fund and the World Bank, and development-oriented nongovernmental organizations. The word donors is used interchangeably with the terms international development community and development cooperation agencies.

PEACEBUILDING. According to the U.N. document *Supplement to an Agenda for Peace* (para. 47), some of the key components of peacebuilding are "demilitarization, the control of small arms, institutional reform, improved police and judicial systems, the monitoring of human rights, electoral reform, and social and economic development."

process. This Policy Essay examines the role that one segment of the international community—the international development community—can play in supporting the efforts of war-torn societies to strengthen their political institutions, restore their economies, repair their social fabric, and consolidate their internal and external security.

Most members of the international development community have been wary of becoming involved in activities that depart from their basic mission of promoting sustainable development. Nevertheless, the share of total official development assistance that provides emergency assistance to countries in conflict or just emerging from conflict has expanded significantly at a time when most aid budgets are shrinking, and donors have recognized that conflict can easily wipe out years of developmental efforts.[1] Many donors now appreciate the importance of supporting efforts to consolidate peace.

Participants in the first peacebuilding efforts operated in largely uncharted territory and were forced to react to events, rather than shape them.[2] Nonetheless, since the beginning of the 1990s, development cooperation agencies have gained valuable experience in addressing the needs of post-conflict countries. In 1994, the Overseas Development Council began a two-year research project that examined peacebuilding efforts in four countries emerging from prolonged periods of internal conflict: Cambodia, El Salvador, Mozambique, and Nicaragua. In collaboration with analysts and nongovernmental organizations (NGOs) in these countries, the project investigated the role that the international development community could play in all steps along the road from war to peace.

The project had three objectives. First, it sought to identify specific steps to be taken by external and local actors to support post-conflict reconstruction, political reconciliation, and renewed development in the countries under study. Second, it considered the appropriate degree and nature of donor involvement in peacebuilding activities, some of which have traditionally fallen outside the purview of development institutions. Third, it examined methods of promoting collaboration among the actors involved in peacebuilding efforts: members of the international development community, multilateral and bilateral political institutions, and governments and private sector actors in war-torn societies.

This essay draws on the experiences of these four countries to derive lessons for the international development community in its efforts to help war-torn countries recover from the ravages of conflict. Part II summarizes the core institutional, economic, social, and security-related characteristics of post-conflict countries and highlights several additional characteristics that influence the interactions between war-torn countries and donors. Part III maps out the phases of the peace process in order to illustrate the ways in which donors can help countries to move from war to peace. It then reviews efforts made by the international development community to strengthen the political institutions of war-torn societies, to consolidate internal and external security, and to promote economic and social revitalization once hostilities end.

Part IV analyzes six lessons derived from the early peacebuilding efforts and explores their implications for the international development community. These lessons are applicable first and foremost to countries with negotiated peace settlements. At the same time, many of the guidelines for donor activities are also germane to situations in which wars end with the victory of one party over another. Part V proposes several next steps for the donors and other members of the international community to improve the quality of the assistance provided to war-torn societies.

Part II
Post-Conflict Countries

. . . .
COMMON FEATURES

■ CIVIL WARS OCCUR IN COUNTRIES AT DIFFERENT levels of political and economic development, with diverse political and social systems, and with varying physical and human resources, cultures, and historical experiences. These countries follow different paths along the road from war to peace, and the international community will need to provide assistance tailored to each country's particular circumstances. Nevertheless, the experience of prolonged internal strife creates fundamental similarities among societies, and these similarities provide the basis on which to construct peacebuilding strategies applicable to a broad spectrum of countries.

Certain political, institutional, economic, social, and security-related features are common to war-torn countries, as are certain characteristics that define the context in which the movement from war to peace occurs. Many of these traits are shared by countries undergoing other types of transformations, such as Central European countries, which are simultaneously liberalizing their political systems and their economies, or the successor states of the Soviet Union, which are combining state building with an economic and political transition. What separates post-conflict societies from these countries is largely a matter of degree. The magnitude of the damage to infrastructure, depletion of human resources, militarization of society, low regime legitimacy, societal disruption, and institutional weakness places war-torn societies on a different plane from societies undergoing relatively peaceful transformations.

. . . .
INSTITUTIONAL CHARACTERISTICS

■ COUNTRIES EMERGING FROM PROLONGED CIVIL WARS display a fundamental paradox. The state is the dominant actor in virtually all sectors, giving it the appearance of substantial capacity. State institutions, however, are weak, ill-suited to the new, post-conflict environment, and incapable of fulfilling the basic functions of government. Efforts to strengthen and restructure the state apparatus so that governments can fulfill roles critical to the efficient functioning of the economy and the political system—such as investing in physical and social infrastructure, maintaining law and order, and fostering economic development—are severely hampered by the political environment following armed conflict. That environment is characterized by a vigorous competition for power that often obscures the need to resolve critical national issues, by political leaders whose legitimacy is weak, by extreme polarization, and by a lack of consensus on the direction in which the country should move.

By its very nature, politics involves a contest for power, but that struggle is particularly acute in post-conflict societies. The mechanisms that would mediate political disputes are either weak or nonexistent, and thus politics becomes the means through which the parties hope to resolve the unfinished business of war. Because political institutions and procedures are poorly developed, the "winner" of the political game expects to be allowed to define the system.

This situation is further complicated by the low regard in which the state and political leaders from all parties and factions are often held. This disaffection derives both from past policies and behavior and from the human costs of the conflict. As a group, post-conflict countries have minimal experience with efficient, representative government. Political parties rarely offer distinct platforms or programs. Rather, they serve as a mechanism for gaining control of the government in order to extract the economic benefits and privileges that have traditionally accrued to rulers. Moreover, the normal realignment of parties that can be expected as authoritarian regimes and wartime coalitions disintegrate distracts politicians from the business of governing.

Certain characteristics of the post-war environment encourage polarization. The armed opposition claims victory because it forced the government to make concessions at the negotiating table, while the government claims victory because it was not defeated on the battlefield. These claims contribute to an unrealistic evaluation of each side's political strength in the period immediately following war. More broadly, regions that were traditionally outposts of support for the opposition tend to remain so, at least in the short term. Severely constrained resources often make it difficult for post-war governments to win popular support.

Finally, although the peace agreement may signify a general consensus that armed combat must end, it does not necessarily represent a common position on the appropriate strategies for the future. The inability of political leaders to focus on substance and their tendency to view events through the lens of power politics impede the development of a national consensus on goals and the setting of priorities.

Addressing these problems, which is a prerequisite for lasting peace, is a lengthy procedure, because few leaders of highly centralized, authoritarian systems willingly cede power, particularly when they retain control over the instruments of violence. Even when reforms are mandated by the peace accords, their implementation is far from certain. Civil society institutions that serve as one means of applying pressure on democratic governments are poorly developed in post-conflict countries. Those civil institutions that exist in the early stages of peacebuilding are often inexperienced and highly politicized, which seriously undermines their effectiveness.

. . . .

ECONOMIC AND SOCIAL TRAITS

■ WARFARE OF THE SORT EXPERIENCED by the countries examined in this essay has significant economic repercussions. On the macro level, economic and social infrastructure—such as the systems for transport and communication, banking, health care, education, and agricultural research and extension—suffers extensive damage as a result of fighting or lack of maintenance. Many basic functions such as transporting goods, communicating from town to town, obtaining health care, or attending school may be disrupted completely.

Moreover, because much of the fighting in civil wars occurs in the countryside, rural economies tend to be hard-hit by conflicts. This is of particular concern, because the agricultural sector plays such a dominant role in the economy of many war-torn countries. The composition of economic output frequently changes during wartime, with the share of manufacturing, construction, transport, and commerce in gross domestic product (GDP) declining and the share of subsistence agriculture expanding.[3] Substantial investments are required to restart production, which the economy is hard-pressed to generate internally.

Post-conflict economies are typically heavily indebted, and war exacerbates this problem. The major war-related sources of debt are expenditures incurred to pursue the war, low tax revenues due to the withdrawal of government from areas of conflict, tax evasion, capital flight, and emigration, as well as the loss of domestic production, which reduces export income and increases imports.[4] Export income is often severely diminished by the difficulty of getting goods to market. As a result of these factors, the economies of countries in conflict tend to contract significantly (see Box 2).[5]

Unsustainably high military budgets constitute an additional drain on resources. Military expenditures frequently continue to absorb a sizable share of the budget even after conflicts end, because the political power of the military remains strong and restructuring the military forces is costly.

On the micro level, conflicts generate serious problems associated with human capital, land, and the environment. Shortages of human resources are particularly severe in war-torn societies due to the death, injury, and emigration of skilled personnel. Individuals with professional

BOX 2. THE EFFECT OF WAR ON THE ECONOMY OF EL SALVADOR

Between 1978, when the economy hit its prewar peak, and 1989, a combination of events—primarily civil war, adverse terms of trade, a contraction of regional markets, and inappropriate economic policies—caused El Salvador's real GDP to decline 11 percent. Real per capita income sank to levels of the early 1960s during the same period, while the export of goods and nonfactor services shrank from 30 to 13 percent of GDP. By the mid-1980s, per capita agricultural production was lower than it had been in 1960.

Sources: World Bank, "Report and Recommendation of the International Bank for Reconstruction and Development to the Executive Directors on a Proposed Second Structural Adjustment Loan (SAL) of US$50 Million to the Republic of El Salvador" (Washington, DC, August 23, 1993), pp. 1–2; World Bank, World Tables 1992 (Baltimore, MD: Johns Hopkins University Press for the World Bank, 1992), pp. 240–41; UNDP, 1993 Annual Report of the Resident Coordinator for El Salvador (San Salvador, 1993), p. 2; and UNDP, Launching New Protagonists in Salvadoran Agriculture (San Salvador, December 1993), p. 28.

training such as doctors, lawyers, teachers, and government officials are often targeted during civil wars. In addition, there are fewer opportunities for education during wartime as schools are closed, and teachers are killed, take up arms, or are otherwise prevented from carrying out their duties. For many students, completing their education takes a back seat to participating in the conflict.[6]

A second problem is related to the gender imbalance that often results from prolonged civil wars. In Cambodia and Rwanda, for example, women account for two-thirds or more of the population, resulting in an unusually large number of female-headed households. Women have long borne a disproportionate burden in developing countries, but in societies where men traditionally own the productive resources, the future of women and of their dependent children is particularly precarious following a conflict. In consequence, the productive capacity of these households is not used fully, which slows the economic recovery.

Access to land can be limited as well. First, the widespread use of land mines may render a considerable amount of territory unusable until the mines are removed, often at a considerable cost.[7] Second, conflicts frequently result in multiple claims to land and other assets, and this duplication has the potential for far-reaching, long-term economic and political dislocation. Agricultural land, houses, and business facilities are frequently abandoned for the duration of the conflict and may be occupied by squatters or taken over and distributed by the state to its supporters. In addition, government officials eager to reap financial benefits sometimes grant commercial concessions to land that is already occupied by family farmers. In the highly contentious political environment that characterizes the move from war to peace, multiple claims are difficult to resolve, but failure to settle them can discourage potential investors from committing themselves to the economy, thereby slowing the economic recovery that is vital to the consolidation of peace.

Environmental degradation is an additional legacy of war. Fragile ecosystems, especially hills and coastal regions, are frequently abused due to the movement of population, the excessive exploitation of natural resources, and the destruction of physical infrastructure.[8] The effects of such war-induced environmental degradation are particularly evident in rural areas, where erosion reduces the productive capacity of the soil and the destruction of watersheds reduces the ability to control water. The effects are particularly severe for small producers, who lack the resources needed to improve the land.

Just as prolonged civil war undermines a country's economic and institutional capacity, it also severely weakens the nation's social fabric: It destroys communities, creates a culture of violence, fosters a sense of impermanence and mistrust that makes collaboration on long-term goals difficult to achieve, impoverishes culture, and engenders psychological trauma. The influx of returnees—refugees, internally displaced persons, and former combatants—can disrupt local society. These persons often have adopted customs that are at odds with traditional behavior in their home communities. Youths have become accustomed to town or city life and frequently have difficulty adjusting to rural conditions. Former combatants, many of whom were forcibly conscripted into military service at an early age, may have no memory of civilian life and very few skills of use to civilian society.

Although the social indicators in many of the countries that have experienced lengthy civil wars were weak prior to the onset of conflict, war-induced destruction and poverty cause them to decline even further. Many post-conflict countries record abysmal rates of infant mortality, illiteracy, malnutrition, access to clean water and sanitation facilities, school enrollment, and so on. Many countries in the bottom 40 percent of the human development index of the U.N. Development Programme (UNDP) owe their ranking in no small measure to the effects of war and conflict.

. . . .

SECURITY CHARACTERISTICS

■ POST-CONFLICT COUNTRIES ARE CHARACTERIZED by bloated security establishments that can no longer be supported by peacetime budgets but remain a major political force, by armed opposition that needs to be disarmed and disbanded, and by an overabundance of small arms.[9] Depending on the terms of the peace agreement, all or some portion of the official and irregular forces will have to be demobilized, and new, peacetime armed forces may need to be created.

In contrast to Western democracies where the armed forces defend against external aggression and the civilian police force handles internal security, in war-torn countries, the police force is frequently controlled by the armed forces, which are primarily concerned with internal security. The security forces often have a long history of human rights abuses, are among the dominant political institutions in society, and may be major players in the economic sphere as well. Civilian institutions are rarely able to hold them accountable; rather, executive, legislative, and judicial agencies are frequently subservient to them.

Furthermore, although politically powerful, security forces are often professionally weak. The police are incapable of guaranteeing law and order, and the armed forces cannot protect the country against external aggression. There is consequently a need to redefine the missions of the different elements of the security forces and to strengthen their capacity to fulfill these missions. Creating a professional, apolitical police force is particularly urgent and challenging in an uncertain political and economic environment.

Post-conflict countries lack a tradition of transparency in military affairs. Civilians in the executive and legislative branches often have an imperfect idea of the size of the security forces, their equipment, and the amount of money they spend annually. Few civilians have the capacity to manage security matters, and there may be no defense ministry. Where defense ministries exist, they are frequently staffed by active duty or retired military officers. Military personnel distrust the motives of civilians, and dialogue between civilians and the military is rare.

. . . .

CONTEXTUAL FEATURES

■   SEVERAL CHARACTERISTICS OF POST-CONFLICT countries define the context in which they move from war to peace and influence how they interact with donors: 1) the effects of war-induced isolation; 2) the influence of peace treaties on the scope and pace of change; and 3) the magnitude and urgency of the problems confronting post-conflict countries.

Civil wars engender various forms of isolation within society. The first is the isolation of the combatant. This is a problem particularly for members of guerrilla forces, especially those who join at an early age and spend long periods of time out of contact with civilian society. Former combatants frequently are ill-equipped for civilian life and have unrealistic expectations about their situation after discharge. A second form of isolation is the separation between the areas in which fighting occurs and the rest of the country. People in zones of conflict are cut off not only from the wider world but also from their own country. After the war, the people who make the decisions that affect the zones of conflict or who implement peace-related programs generally did not reside in those areas during the war and may not understand conditions there. The final form of isolation is the separation of these countries from the international system. To varying degrees, post-conflict countries face a learning curve for dealing with donors and other international institutions.[10] Fragile governments are expected to deal with numerous donors and competing recommendations, which complicates the process of adjudicating competing demands.

The impact of each of these forms of isolation can be intensified by the monopoly over information that is exercised by parties to the conflict. Control over the media and the absence of offsetting sources of information enable the parties to create and maintain significant distortions of the truth during the conflict and into the peacebuilding period as well.

In countries that have ended their conflicts through negotiated peace agreements, the scope and pace of the early stages of the transition is determined largely by the provisions of the peace accords and their timetables for implementation. Although timetables are frequently revised and new agreements struck on how to interpret specific provisions, institutional changes such as developing an electoral system, restructuring the security forces, and reforming the judicial branch of government that might, under different circumstances, take considerably longer to effect, must occur on a specific timetable within a year or two following the cessation of hostilities.

Finally, post-conflict countries face a particularly large and complex set of issues that must be addressed rapidly. Economic reform and political liberalization, each of which is potentially destabilizing, have to be carried out while a fragile peace is being consolidated. The requirements of each of the processes may conflict with those of another. For example, the demands of political reconciliation may be at odds with the demands of market reconstruction and the creation of open democratic processes. Finding the correct balance among these objectives is extremely challenging in countries with severely constrained human resources. Doing so takes on heightened urgency because these constraints are often related, in one way or another, to the conflict. Failing to resolve these issues in a timely fashion may create the conditions for a return to organized violence.

Part III
The Peace Process

PHASES OF THE PEACE PROCESS

■   CIVIL WARS END EITHER WITH THE VICTORY of one party or through negotiated settlement. The case studies that provide the basis for this essay are of conflicts that terminate with no outright victor, and Table 1 shows the four phases through which the peace process moves in such circumstances.[11] The length of each phase varies according to the situation in each country. Movement from one phase to the next is not automatic, as the numerous false starts toward peace in countries such as Angola, Liberia, and Rwanda underscore.

The first stage of the peace process—conflict resolution—aims at reaching agreement on key issues so that fighting can stop. This stage has two phases: negotiation and the formal cessation of hostilities. In this stage, international actors have sought to assist the parties to overcome their differences, put diplomatic pressure on the parties, and offered technical assistance in specific areas under negotiation, such as the separation of forces. The compromises necessary to produce a document acceptable to all parties generally leave many key issues wholly or partly unresolved.

The second stage—peacebuilding—consists of two phases: transition and consolidation. Priorities during these two phases center on strengthening political institutions, reforming internal and external security arrangements, and revitalizing the economy and the nation's social fabric. International actors have supported these goals through diplomacy, financial support, and technical assistance. During the transition phase, efforts are made to establish a government with sufficient domestic and international legitimacy to operate effectively and to set in motion key reforms mandated by the peace accords.

Many peace accords, including those in Cambodia, El Salvador, and Mozambique, establish transition periods that last between one and two years and conclude with general elections. It is becoming evident, however, that this time frame is too short for the multiplicity of reforms prescribed by the peace accords to be implemented. What is more, the content of the accords is strongly affected by the balance of forces within the country and has a profound influence on the evolution of that balance.

TABLE 1. PEACE PROCESS IN COUNTRIES WITH NEGOTIATED PEACE SETTLEMENTS

Stages	Conflict Resolution		Peacebuilding	
Phases	*Negotiation*	*Cessation of hostilities*	*Transition*	*Consolidation*
Main Objectives	Agreement on key issues to enable fighting to stop	Signature of peace accords; cease-fire/separation/concentration of forces	Establish a government with adequate legitimacy to rule effectively; begin reforms in the areas of political institution building and post-conflict security; inaugurate economic and social revitalization efforts	Continue and deepen reform process; continue economic/social recovery programs

This can affect outcomes in ways contrary to the terms or intent of the peace agreements.[12] Issues that create sticking points during negotiations often continue to cause difficulties during implementation of the accords.

During the consolidation phase, the reform process continues. The provisions of the peace accord rarely deal adequately with the problems that led to the war or create an environment conducive to resolving conflicts peacefully in the future. Therefore, during the consolidation phase, fundamental economic and social grievances have to be addressed, whether they are enshrined in the peace agreement or not.

. . . .

THE ELEMENTS OF PEACEBUILDING

■ THE INTERNATIONAL COMMUNITY has come to recognize that warring parties require assistance not only in negotiating peace agreements but also in sustaining and consolidating the peace. To implement peace accords, the parties to the conflict must act on many fronts: disarming and demobilizing former combatants, reintegrating demobilized soldiers, demilitarizing police forces, restructuring and reforming the security sector, enforcing respect for human rights, resettling refugees, reforming the judicial system, holding elections, and promoting economic and social revitalization. The parties' capacity to meet these demands is, however, severely constrained by institutional weaknesses, limited human and financial resources, and economic fragility. In consequence, the parties have frequently turned to the international community for financial and technical assistance as well as political support.

In view of the broad range of activities that comprise peacebuilding, a wide variety of external actors provides support: regional and international political bodies, international peacekeeping operations, representatives of the ministries of defense and foreign affairs of friendly countries, multilateral and bilateral donors, and NGOs. The following sections describe areas in which the donors and associated NGOs have played a role in recent peace efforts. For the purpose of this discussion, donor activities are grouped in three categories: 1) those that build political institutions, 2) those that consolidate internal and external security, and

3) those that promote economic and social revitalization. This grouping does not reflect any priority ranking among activities.

BUILDING POLITICAL INSTITUTIONS

Civil wars arise out of a complex combination of economic, social, and political imbalances, with disputes over access to the levers of political power being paramount. Because the institutions capable of mediating these disputes in both the public sectors and civil society are typically either very weak or nonexistent, institutional strengthening is an important aspect of peacebuilding in post-conflict countries.

ELECTORAL PROCESS. A major objective of peacebuilding is to install a government that the country's population and the international community consider legitimate enough to function effectively. Establishing such a government is a first step toward addressing one of the root causes of the conflict and makes an important contribution to fostering national reconciliation. The international community has strongly promoted elections for two reasons. First, elections allow citizens to select their leaders. Second, they clarify the persons and organizations with whom external actors should collaborate. In consequence, elections have come to be seen as the culmination of the peace process and as one of the principal vehicles for achieving reconciliation in countries such as Angola, Cambodia, El Salvador, Haiti, Mozambique, Nicaragua, and South Africa. Virtually all post-conflict countries hold presidential or legislative elections at the end of the transition phase; some hold provincial or municipal elections as well.

Because many of these countries either have no history of elections or have never held elections that are genuinely inclusive and free of intimidation and other flaws, the donors have provided substantial electoral support. This includes assistance in writing or revising electoral laws, amending constitutions, establishing or reforming mechanisms to guide the electoral process, organizing the election, registering voters, and providing voter education.

THE LIMITATIONS OF ELECTIONS. In war-torn countries, elections frequently fail to produce the outcomes that external actors seek. In established democracies, elections are the most satisfactory method of resolving the question of governmental legitimacy. In the post-conflict environment, however, they often do little more than confer a degree of legitimacy on the newly elected government, and they invariably contribute to political polarization in the short term. This outcome is particularly evident in societies without the tradition of a loyal opposition, separation of powers, or officials who serve the public rather than rule over them and where hostility and mistrust are strong.

Moreover, when the results of elections are not enforced, when they are manipulated, or when participation in the electoral process does not translate into participation in governing, reconciliation is undermined (see Box 3). One solution has been to create a government of national unity. The apparent success of this model in South Africa has encouraged the international community to support its adoption in other post-conflict situations. Reaching agreement on this alternative may depend, however, on the existence of an internal political dynamic that is rarely found in the aftermath of prolonged conflicts. Reaching power-sharing agreements during peace negotiations may be extremely difficult, while trying to graft this mechanism onto peace accords in the run-up to national elections may be counterproductive.

BOX 3. CAMBODIAN ELECTION AND RECONCILIATION

In Cambodia in May 1993, the main opposition party, the United Front for an Independent, Neutral, Peaceful, and Cooperative Cambodia (FUNCINPEC), won a plurality of the vote (45 percent) and 58 seats in the National Assembly. Nonetheless, the party ruling before the election, the Cambodian People's Party (CPP), parlayed 38 percent of the vote and 51 seats into a coalition government with FUNCINPEC. It accomplished this by exploiting the fear of secession—threatened by "dissident" high-ranking members of the CPP—of eight eastern provinces bordering on Vietnam and other acts of intimidation.

A coalition government might well have been the logical outcome of the electoral process in any case, given the relative administrative, military, and financial strengths of the two parties. In common with opposition parties in other countries that are just setting out on the road to establishing multiparty political systems, FUNCINPEC was clearly unable to govern by itself. However, the method by which the coalition was achieved and the fact that the elections did little, if anything, to make the government accountable to the electorate established bad precedents and potentially damaged the process of reconciliation.

Another possibility worth exploring is to phase in elected, representative government over a longer period of time, perhaps as long as five years. During this period, an interim caretaker government would be established. The executive branch would be headed by a respected public figure and appointed ministers. These individuals would be sought from among the ranks of the major political groupings and technocrats at home and abroad. Elections would first be held for a constituent assembly and subsequently for a permanent legislature and chief executive. During the transition period, intensive efforts would be needed to establish the foundation on which representative government could be constructed.

At present, because so much rides on elections in post-conflict societies, the international community, including the donors, has focused on ensuring that elections take place. Once elections have occurred and a new government is in place, the international community begins to pay more attention to other activities such as enhancing participation through decentralization of government responsibility and authority, reforming the civil service, improving the efficacy of the legislature, strengthening civil society (including political parties), and finding an appropriate role for traditional authorities. If the transition phase were lengthened, more consideration could be given to these critical components of political development before elections are held, so that the institutional base would be stronger when voting occurred.

RESPECT FOR HUMAN RIGHTS. One of the hallmarks of prolonged, low-intensity civil wars is the widespread violation of human rights. In many cases, such violations occurred before the onset of armed conflict and contributed to the decision to take up arms. The failure to respect human rights occurs first and foremost because the structures that prevent the state security forces from acting with impunity are either weak or nonexistent.

Human rights protection relies on the existence and enforcement of laws that regulate the behavior of state security forces. It depends on reform of the security sector as well as the creation or strengthening of a legal system that settles disputes systematically and of a judicial system that treats all citizens equally and fairly. Yet the legal framework and the capacity to enforce laws after a prolonged conflict are often quite limited. Human rights protection requires the establishment of countervailing forces, both within government—for example, the Office of the National Counsel for the Defense of Human Rights mandated by the El Salvador peace accords—and within civil society—such as the numerous human rights groups that were funded by the United Nations during the transition phase in Cambodia.

The truth commission is a popular mechanism for helping societies to overcome the trauma of years of systematic violence. Although some post-conflict governments have argued that linking individuals with specific acts of violence impedes reconciliation, others have argued that it is vital to know the truth about all abuses to avoid repeating the past. Although the truth commission can raise sensitive issues and assist society as a whole to come to terms with past abuses, several conditions need to be met if it is to promote national healing.

The process needs to be generated and supported internally. External actors should not drive or play a major role in the process, as happened, for example, with the truth commission in El Salvador (see Box 4). External actors can, however, provide information on the strengths and weaknesses of different models of such commissions. They can also offer material support, for example, by lending the commission office space or equipment. Finally, truth commissions may be only the first step in a process that takes many steps and many years to complete. In Argentina and Chile, admissions of guilt and of involvement in illegal practices continued to surface many years after formal inquiries were completed.

As a group, donors have supported a broad range of activities designed to enhance the respect for human rights. They have also supported truth commissions and the establishment of new institutions in both the governmental and nongovernmental sectors.

CONSOLIDATING INTERNAL AND EXTERNAL SECURITY

The signing of the peace accords sets in motion a series of activities in the security sector designed to terminate hostilities: permanent ceasefire, separation of forces, and concentration of forces in preparation for

The Mexico Agreements of April 27, 1991, between the Government of El Salvador and the Frente Farabundo Martí para la Liberación Nacional (FMLN), set up the Commission on the Truth to investigate human rights abuses in El Salvador between 1980 and 1991. The three commissioners were well respected internationally, but none was a Salvadoran citizen. The commission's report, *From Madness to Hope: The 12-Year War in El Salvador,* was made public on March 15, 1993. Its recommendations included significant judicial reform, the dismissal of certain public officials from their posts and a ten-year ban on holding elective office for others, the construction of a national monument bearing the names of victims, and the creation of a compensation fund. However, the commission had no power to enforce the implementation of its recommendations. The FMLN accepted the report's recommendations in their entirety despite reservations. In contrast, although El Salvador's president, Alfredo Cristiani, pledged to comply with the recommendations if they met certain criteria, such as constitutionality and compatibility with the peace accords, he urged the National Assembly to approve a general amnesty pardoning individuals implicated in wartime abuses. The assembly did so on March 20, 1993, thereby short-circuiting the development of a national consensus on the desirability of an amnesty.

Source: United Nations, The United Nations and El Salvador, 1990–1995, *Blue Book Series 4 (New York: United Nations, Department of Public Information, 1995).*

demobilizing excess personnel. As part of this process, inventories of weapons are compiled, their completeness is verified by neutral bodies, and individual soldiers are disarmed. Much of the responsibility for these activities lies with regional or international political and military bodies. Donors have, however, supported cantoned soldiers, particularly those belonging to the armed opposition. In addition, because the disarmament provisions of the peace agreements frequently are complied with only partially, weapons buyback schemes have become attractive in recent years, and countries have asked donors to support such efforts.

To ensure that the gains of the initial phases of the peace process are preserved and to lay the foundation for political liberalization and sustainable development, peacebuilding efforts should also include reform of the security sector. In some instances, the peace accords mandate specific reforms, but more often they merely lay out political objectives in which these reforms are implicit. Donors have offered limited support for these broad objectives.

CANTONMENT. Soldiers are cantoned as part of post-conflict demobilization for political and security reasons: to ensure that all combatants and their weapons are accounted for and to build confidence that each side will maintain its commitments. The precise needs of cantoned troops vary considerably. If troops are confined to barracks, which most government troops are, they may have minimal need for additional shelter, food, clothing, sanitation facilities, and medical care. Nevertheless, some governments, which often owe their troops substantial back pay, may not be able to provide for soldiers' basic needs during cantonment. Opposition forces typically require that everything be provided for them, and this assistance is often needed urgently (see Table 2). In addition, cantoned soldiers may have special health care needs, particularly members of the opposition who have lived for years without proper medical attention.[13]

Equally important, because of their political context, demobilization programs are subject to special conditions and unanticipated delays. Opposition forces are reluctant to disband because they lose their only

TABLE 2. SUPPORT TO ENCAMPED FMLN SOLDIERS

Category of Assistance	Assistance Provided
Basic infrastructure	Temporary shelters, potable water systems, latrines, dining areas, kitchens, health care centers
Primary health care	Equipment for health care centers, medical examinations, laboratory analyses, dental treatment, specialized treatment (cardiology, dermatology, general surgery, physiotherapy, psychiatry), training in the prevention of illnesses
Food aid	Supply, storage, and distribution of basic and supplemental food
Basic education	Basic education and evaluation, literacy training, preparation of candidates for National Academy of Public Security examinations, limited secondary education

Source: United Nations Development Programme, Regional Bureau for Latin America and the Caribbean, Final Progress Report: Emergency Programme for Persons in Process of Demobilization in El Salvador *(New York: UNDP, February 1993).*

means of pressuring the government. Government forces may be reluctant to disband for psychological reasons (demobilization places them on a par with the enemy and forces them to adjust to a new situation about which they feel considerable unease) as well as for political reasons (the military equates political power with the number of men under arms). As the cantonment period is extended, provisioning the encamped soldiers becomes more costly, and new needs are created. For example, it is often necessary to provide basic medical assistance and other services to the families of encamped soldiers as well as to civilians living nearby.

Donors often face legal restrictions on the use of funds to support active duty military personnel, which can complicate their ability to provide assistance to cantoned soldiers. These restrictions can frequently be overcome, for example, through special waivers, although this can be a time-consuming process. It can also lead to seemingly arbitrary decisions, such as when USAID refused to support Mozambican army medical doctors because they were active duty military personnel, even though they were providing medical care to soldiers awaiting demobilization.

WEAPONS BUYBACKS. Disarmament of former combatants is a central feature of all peace processes. Soldiers are typically required to hand in at least one weapon upon entering an official troop assembly point, and mechanisms are established to account for and dispose of all weapons belonging to the parties to the conflict. However, these mechanisms do not eliminate excess weapons, because most soldiers have more than one weapon and military organizations frequently maintain hidden stocks of weapons as a hedge against breakdown of the peace process. In addition, private citizens and members of paramilitary groups, who are rarely subject to formal demobilization processes, frequently have substantial stocks of weapons. Supplementary disarmament efforts, particularly weapons buyback schemes, are one approach that governments have considered to reduce the number of weapons in circulation.

Key to the success of buyback programs is the existence of adequate employment opportunities, a civil police force capable of creating a secure environment in which the value of weapons decreases, as well as regional efforts to stem the arms trade. Among the elements believed to increase the chances of success are the following: 1) the existence of numerous collection points, including mobile teams in rural areas; 2) a clear description of the terms of purchase, procedures for turning in weapons, and duration of the program; 3) a policy of purchasing only working weapons; 4) immediate destruction or secure storage of the weapons purchased; 5) efforts to create peer pressure to turn in weapons, including information campaigns and group returns; and 6) a purchase price that is set below the commercial price but above the black market price.[14]

In general, weapons buyback schemes have not reduced significantly the number of weapons in circulation. In large part this is because guns move easily across borders in regions of long-standing conflicts such as Central America and Southern Africa. Moreover, programs that incorporate all of the critical features described above are difficult to design and implement. Not unreasonably, donor agencies have been reluctant to finance weapons buybacks. A new approach, which has been proposed for El Salvador, focuses on providing communities with the incentives to control the possession and influx of weapons. Both the Canadian and Spanish governments have expressed interest in funding this project. If successfully implemented, it could provide a model for future buyback efforts. However, even if the Salvadoran government agrees to proceed with the program, its outcome will not be known for some time.

SECURITY SECTOR REFORMS. Security forces have traditionally played a central role in the political and economic life of developing countries. Repressive regimes, backed or controlled by security forces, were a major cause of the armed conflict in several of the countries whose experiences form the core of this analysis. Civil wars greatly enhance the power and autonomy of security forces vis-à-vis civilians both in the general population and in government.

For security forces to make the transition to democratic rule and to eliminate the political, social, and economic abuses that spawned armed conflict, several reforms are necessary. Some are specifically mandated by the peace agreements; others are implicit in the requirements imposed by the peace treaties (see Box 5). All are vital for consolidating the peace. Reforms that have been part of the peace process in the four countries studied here include the following: 1) redefining the doctrine and missions

BOX 5. PEACE ACCORDS ON REFORM OF THE SECURITY SECTOR

EL SALVADOR. Of the four peace accords examined in detail for this essay, the El Salvador peace accords were by far the most inclusive and explicit in their reform of the security sector. Among its numerous security provisions, the Chapultepec Treaty clearly delineated how responsibility for internal and external security would be divided, defined the doctrine of both the Armed Forces of El Salvador (FAES) and the new National Civil Police (PNC), established a procedure for vetting the past performance of all members of the FAES and ending impunity on the part of the FAES, reaffirmed civilian control of the security forces, laid out the structure of the PNC and the National Public Security Academy, and described the criteria and mechanisms for selecting and training police officers.

MOZAMBIQUE. The Mozambique accords focused primarily on the mechanisms for creating a unified armed forces and described the bare bones of the structure of the new force. They also described the mission of the Mozambican Defense Force (FADM) and stated that the force would be "nonpartisan, career, professionally trained, and competent, . . . made up exclusively . . . of volunteers . . . drawn from the forces of both Parties. . . . [and] preclude all forms of racial or ethnic discrimination or discrimination based on language or religious affiliation." The provisions relating to the police force were no more detailed.

CAMBODIA. The Cambodian peace accords were completely silent on the subject of reforming the security sector.

NICARAGUA. The Central American peace process that set in motion the end to the war between the Nicaraguan government and the U.S.-backed *contras* was very general, calling for "democratiation" but offering no specifics on the role and structure of military forces in the signatory countries. Nonetheless, the Nicaraguan army is progressively being reformed. On September 2, 1994, Nicaragua adopted the Code of Military Organization, Jurisdiction, and Social Security. This laid the basis for greater civilian control over the military, granting the president the power to appoint and remove the chief of the armed forces, clearly stating the apolitical and non-partisan nature of the armed forces, and circumscribing to some degree the right of the armed forces to raise and spend money.

These were, however, modest reforms, both in the rights ceded by the military to the civilian authorities and the adjustments that remain to be made. For example, although the president can appoint the chief of the armed forces, the military proposes the candidates. And although the army no longer controls business enterprises, that control now resides in the Military Social Security Institute, which administers the army's social security system. Furthermore, the code specifies that one of the army's missions is to support the national police in maintaining internal security.

of the security forces, including a clear separation of internal and external security functions and the primacy of civilian control; 2) restructuring the security forces in line with the new doctrines, missions, and budgetary realities, which almost invariably leads to some degree of downsizing; 3) evaluating officers who intend to serve in the post-conflict armed forces; 4) reforming the military and police education systems to stress the goals of democratic societies; 5) disbanding paramilitary forces; and 6) terminating extralegal forms of recruiting security forces.

Foreign countries have supported many of these efforts through their foreign and defense ministries and civilian law enforcement agencies, as well as through development cooperation agencies. In general, however, the donors have not accorded these fundamental reforms the attention they merit. Part IV outlines specific ways in which donors might assist governments of war-torn countries to meet these objectives.

PROMOTING ECONOMIC AND SOCIAL REVITALIZATION

Countries that have suffered prolonged civil wars face enormous economic and social deficits. Although foreign assistance was initially developed to support the economic recovery of European countries after World War II, recent rehabilitation and reconstruction efforts have focused on helping countries to overcome physical disasters, such as floods and droughts. The definitions of rehabilitation and reconstruction developed in this context are broadly applicable to post-war situations. *Rehabilitation* aims to restore individuals and their communities to self-sufficiency. This includes activities such as emergency repairs to physical infrastructure and the provision of seeds, housing materials, and simple agricultural or construction tools. *Reconstruction* seeks to restore communities to their preexisting status or perhaps even move beyond their preexisting status.[15]

Donors have been asked to provide assistance for assessing damage to economic and social infrastructure; rehabilitating and reconstructing basic infrastructure such as health and education services, water and sanitation systems, the banking system, and communications infrastructure (roads, bridges, telecommunications facilities); implementing environmental awareness and protection programs (soil conservation, flood control, reforestation, wildlife management); reactivating the smallholder agricultural sector; rehabilitating export agriculture; and providing housing and technical assistance.

Although the definition of rehabilitation and reconstruction may be applicable to different types of disasters, the programs developed need to be tailored closely to conditions in the post-conflict environment. For example, rebuilding following natural disasters focuses on reconstructing infrastructure, while rebuilding after a prolonged conflict covers a wide spectrum of activities. In particular, attention should be given to restoring both the nation's social fabric and its human resource capacity. A special challenge for post-conflict countries is the degree to which the objective should be *construction* rather than reconstruction, both to maximize the productive capacity of the economy and to support reconciliation. Plans to repair damaged hospitals, health clinics, schools, sewage and water systems, and electricity grids are important, but they do not address the needs of war-affected populations in areas where no such services ever existed.[16]

Two needs that are essential to promoting economic and social recovery in war-torn countries are reintegrating the groups most affected by war and mine clearance.

REINTEGRATION OF THE MOST WAR-AFFECTED GROUPS. Civil wars disrupt the lives of all citizens, but some groups suffer disproportionately. Particularly disadvantaged groups include persons who are forced to leave their homes, soldiers and their dependents, child soldiers, female-headed households, orphans, and individuals suffering the physical and psychological wounds of war.

During wars, refugees often depend heavily on relief aid for their survival, because access to land and other forms of employment are limited. This dependence can lead, among other things, to a loss of skills and initiative, undermining their capacity to reestablish themselves and their families once the war is over. Persons who have been internally displaced experience many of the same problems. Female combatants, the wives of male veterans, and widows face social and economic constraints and burdens that derive to a large extent from the traditional role of women in these societies. If not overcome, these can cause considerable hardship for women and their children.

Most soldiers leave the military with minimal education, few peacetime skills, no access to land and other productive resources, and few if any savings. Many are physically and psychologically handicapped by the war and find it difficult to take independent initiatives and cope with the ordinary demands of civilian life. Adding to these problems, civilian society is frequently wary of former combatants. Even when they do possess marketable skills, such as those of a mechanic or a driver, many demobilized soldiers have little or no experience in the labor market, having taken up arms at an early age. They also tend to have an imperfect understanding of the state of the economy. Demobilized soldiers often have unrealistic assumptions about what civilian life can offer and require a period of adjustment in which to assess their personal situation and options. These characteristics are particularly relevant for members of the armed opposition and for foot soldiers, whose opportunities for education and personal advancement are more limited than those of the officer corps (see Table 3).

Child soldiers, some of whom are orphans or have been separated from their families for many years, are especially vulnerable at the end of conflicts, since the breakup of the wartime group is akin to losing their family for a second time. Moreover, some armed groups deny that they have children in their ranks, thereby preventing child soldiers from receiv-

TABLE 3. PROFILE OF SECURITY FORCE PERSONNEL RECEIVING REINTEGRATION BENEFITS IN EL SALVADOR (years)

Characteristic	FMLN	FAES	National Civil Police
Average age	20–22	24	26
Average length of service	4–5	2	—
Average length of education	6	5	9

Note:—is not available.
Source: USAID/El Salvador, "The First Three Years of the Peace and National Recovery Project (519-0394): Lessons Learned" (San Salvador: Office of Infrastructure and Regional Development, October 1994), app. D.

ing assistance. Nonetheless, efforts have been made to identify child sol-diers early in the demobilization process and then to remove them from the cantonment areas and reunite them with their families. Even those who are older than eighteen at the time of demobilization may need special assistance because they have not experienced civilian life as adults.

Donors and NGOs have traditionally focused on facilitating the return of refugees and on providing assistance to refugees and the inter-nally displaced once they have returned to their communities. Assistance to war-affected civilians and to residents of geographic regions designated as most war-affected has included temporary food packages, materials for rebuilding houses, access to land, production credits, assistance to the physically handicapped, specific health interventions such as medi-cal vaccines, accreditation of educational and labor skills, replacement of lost personal documentation, short-term vocational training, and job-creation projects.

In contrast, donors have tended to be considerably less enthusias-tic about assisting former combatants, who are held responsible for uproot-ing tens or hundreds of thousands, if not millions, of people from their homes and causing considerable loss of life, destruction of physical infra-structure, and suffering. Nonetheless, peace agreements often specify such assistance, and, from a political standpoint, it may be very difficult to avoid extending aid to demobilized soldiers in view of their capacity to disrupt the peace process. Some form of reintegration program exists or will be formed in countries such as Angola, Cambodia, El Salvador, Eritrea, Ethiopia, Haiti, Liberia, Mozambique, Namibia, and Nicaragua.[17]

As a result, more and more donors are providing former combat-ants and their families with two types of support: an initial reinsertion package that functions as a temporary safety net and longer-term reinte-gration assistance aimed at helping them to become involved in productive activities over the longer term (see Box 6). Reinsertion programs have sought to provide veterans with the basic necessities of life—shelter, medical care, food, clothing, and household goods—and with transport to their home district. In addition, some reinsertion programs have provided special medical assistance and support for physically handicapped veter-ans. Rarely have they dealt with psychological problems.

Refugees, internally displaced persons, and demobilized soldiers have similar needs, and more and more donors agree that long-term

The experience of former combatants in El Salvador underlines the importance of providing short-term reinsertion assistance to demobilized soldiers.

■ Members of the FMLN received no severance pay or other immediate assistance once they were demobilized and left official troop assembly areas. Rather, it was assumed that they would benefit from the land transfer program established by the peace accords and begin farming immediately following demobilization. This assumption proved problematic in several important respects. First, some former FMLN soldiers did not want to become farmers at all. Second, delays in implementing the transfer of land meant that land was not immediately available for the vast majority who did want to farm. Third, many former FMLN soldiers and officers lacked a social safety net because they had no families to whom they could turn for support until they either received land or found some alternative employment. As a result vocational training programs were developed, but many former combatants participated in these programs largely to obtain the stipends provided to trainees.

■ Former members of the FAES experienced considerable difficulty accessing the benefits promised to them, including land, credits, and severance pay. Some were frustrated to the point of forming a political pressure group, which has led violent demonstrations that have increased societal tensions.

reintegration programs should be linked with community-based rehabilitation and reconstruction efforts. Up to now, however, most veteran assistance has been targeted solely to the former combatants themselves and has included cash payments, job and psychological counseling, vocational training, apprenticeships, formal education, job creation, support for job search, access to land, credits, technical assistance, and support in identifying market needs.

MINE CLEARANCE. Traditionally a defensive weapon, land mines have been employed in an offensive capacity in low-intensity conflicts over the last 35 years or so. Compared with other weapons, mines are extremely inexpensive. They are readily acquired through international trade and are easily manufactured locally. The development of scatterable mines, which can be delivered by aircraft, artillery, or tank-borne weapons, has escalated both the offensive use of land mines and the difficulty of mapping mine fields. In addition, because scatterable mines are relatively small and have limited explosive power, they tend to be sown closely

BOX 7. MINE CLEARANCE IN CAMBODIA

Mines were widely used in Cambodia, and an estimated 8 to 10 million were still in place in 1995 in an area covering 3,200 square kilometers. Land mines have taken a heavy toll. At the war's end, the International Committee of the Red Cross estimated that there were more than 30,000 amputees in Cambodia: 1 in every 236 Cambodians had lost at least one limb. In 1994, more than 300 Cambodians were killed or injured by mines each month.

The U.N. Transitional Authority Cambodia (UNTAC) helped Cambodian officials to establish the Cambodian Mine-Action Center (CMAC) in April 1992. UNTAC also established the Mine Clearance Training Unit, which was merged with CMAC in July 1993. CMAC is responsible for the full range of demining activities: awareness, marking, and clearance of mines as well as training to clear mines. In mid-1994 CMAC employed 1,500 Cambodian deminers. Once the UNTAC mandate ended, the UNDP assumed responsibility for coordinating international funding for CMAC through a trust fund. Between 1993 and 1995, the international community supplied 30 technical advisers who worked with 20 Cambodians to manage CMAC's operations. The intention was to phase out the international advisers by early 1996. Four NGOs—Halo Trust, Handicap International, Mine Advisory Group, and Norwegian People's Aid—have collaborated with CMAC in demining activities. The U.N. Children's Fund (UNICEF) has supported mine awareness training.

CMAC is developing a village demining program in which instructors teach selected villagers to detect and mark mines. Removal remains the responsibility of trained deminers. CMAC is also developing mobile teams to conduct mine awareness training.

Although constrained by resources, CMAC and its collaborators had cleared more than 10 million square kilometers of land by April 1994, destroying 25,000 antipersonnel mines, some 150 antitank mines, and nearly 140,000 pieces of unexploded ordnance. Of CMAC's $20 million budget for 1993–95, the international community pledged $11.6 million.

Sources: U.N. General Assembly, Assistance in Mine Clearance: Report of the Secretary-General, A/49/357 *(New York: United Nations, September 6, 1994), p. 16; Office of International Security and Peacekeeping Operations*, Hidden Killers: The Global Land Mine Crisis, 1994 Report to the U.S. Congress on the Problem with Uncleared Land Mines and the United States Strategy for Demining and Land Mine Control, *Publication No. 10225 (Washington, DC: Bureau of Political-Military Affairs, U.S. Department of State, December 1994), pp. 46–47.*

together, making them all the more dangerous to civilian populations. Mines are used heavily in wars that seek to terrorize civilians.

As a result, the removal of land mines is now an integral part of the end of every civil war (see Box 7). Demining is crucial to return land to productive uses, to enhance the free circulation of people and goods, and to enable peacekeepers and aid workers to carry out their tasks. In general, demining is conducted initially by foreign military personnel, firms, and NGOs. The objective almost always is to develop an indigenous capacity to demine. Deminers need to know how to identify and locate mines, map mine fields, and mark and clear mines.

Another crucial aspect of demining programs is mine awareness training for the public. According to the U.S. Department of State, it is extremely important that mine awareness programs "not be divorced or performed in isolation from" the process of removing mines. Local populations can identify the location of mines, can benefit from knowing the location of mine fields, and need to understand the importance of not interfering with the work of deminers.[18] Returning refugees and internally displaced persons are particularly at risk of injury and death from mines, both on the road home or near their villages.

Demining activities during recent transitions have been relatively popular with donors, particularly bilateral ones. In a number of instances, the U.N. Department of Humanitarian Affairs and UNDP have managed demining trust funds for the international community.

Part IV
The Lessons of Peacebuilding

....
LESSONS FROM EXPERIENCE

"The peace and national recovery project is in one sense unique: how often is the U.S. economic aid program involved in supporting the demobilization of armed forces? How often does it need to deal with parties who have just quit fighting each other?"

—Development Associates, Inc., *Final Report: Evaluation of the Peace and National Recovery Project, El Salvador*[19]

■   FAR FROM BEING ISOLATED EVENTS, the many peace processes currently under way have much to teach the international development community about a category of assistance that it is increasingly being called on to provide aid in countries emerging from protracted civil wars. Six key lessons about the scope and delivery of this assistance have emerged from ODC's examination of recent peacebuilding efforts.

■ Constraints on the scope, design, and delivery of relief and long-term development assistance make necessary a new form of aid for the transition phase of the peace process: post-conflict transition assistance.

■ The international donor community has an important role to play during all four phases of the peace process. Donors should be involved from the negotiation through the consolidation phase.

■ A fundamental reform of the security sector is critical to the ultimate consolidation of peace. In collaboration with other members of the international community, donors should promote security sector reform vigorously during all phases of the peace process.

■ Because peacebuilding activities are inherently political and are implemented in highly politicized environments, the selection, design, and implementation of programs cannot be approached from a purely technical perspective. Political considerations can both improve and detract from a program's quality, and donors should work to minimize the negative effects and maximize the positive ones.

■ Donors urgently need to consider how external assistance can best be used to strengthen the government's capacity to perform key tasks during the transition phase without bolstering its capacity to use resources for partisan political purposes. Restarting government has rarely received the attention it deserves given the extreme weakness of the public sector in countries emerging from prolonged internal conflicts.

- Civil wars create the conditions in which fundamental political and economic restructuring can occur. To capitalize on the fairly short window of opportunity that exists for effecting significant change, coordination among the relevant actors is crucial.

This part explores these lessons, giving particular emphasis to their implication for the activities of the international donor community at each stage of the peace process.

. . . .

POST-CONFLICT TRANSITION ASSISTANCE

"The end of the cold war has ... created more so-called transitional situations ... where timely provision of assistance can help revitalize society, reinforce institutions, and preserve national order. These countries have special needs that are not addressed by traditional disaster relief or long-term programs of sustainable development. ... Transitional nations are often poised simultaneously for either growth or chaos. Given the opportunities and the risks—especially from the failure to act quickly and effectively—the donor community must try to respond."

—USAID, "Providing Humanitarian Assistance and Aiding Post-Crisis Transitions: USAID's Strategy"[20]

■ OF THE FOUR PHASES OF THE PEACE PROCESS, the transition phase places the greatest sustained demands on the resources of the participants, both external and local. The international community has offered intensive diplomatic, financial, military, and technical assistance between the time the peace treaty is signed and general elections are held. This assistance has come from a variety of institutions: development cooperation agencies, including the multilateral development banks and U.N. agencies; foreign, defense, and justice ministries; nongovernmental and private international organizations; and the private sector.

The donors have been able to draw on two forms of assistance during the transition phase: emergency aid and development assistance. Neither of these is particularly well suited to the specific needs generated during this period. Development financing is encumbered by numerous regulations that slow the delivery of resources, and development projects typically take several years to come on line. Peace processes cannot, however, wait for donors to go through normal channels. Relief assistance is more accessible but was developed as a means of responding to natural disasters and has a limited time frame. Once the emergency is over, this category of funding is phased out. The emergency period is not necessarily coterminous with the transition phase.

In addition, peacebuilding requires supporting objectives that have not traditionally been within the purview of either relief or development assistance. For example, many donors cannot employ relief funds for activities that do not save lives. This means that relief aid often cannot be used for rehabilitation, such as restoring the educational system or reconstructing houses. For their part, development practitioners tend to view certain aspects of peacebuilding, such as consolidating internal and external security, as a distraction from the goals of promoting sustainable development and creating sound economic policies and structures and are loath to use their money to support such activities.

Finally, because the toll exacted by war on human and institutional resources can significantly impede progress in war-torn countries, project benchmarks and performance targets for regular development programs are frequently inappropriate or too stringent. For example, the resources invested in reintegration programs for former combatants have often not been intended primarily to guarantee the beneficiaries a sustained livelihood. Rather, they have been intended to provide the former soldiers with a breathing space to adjust to civilian life and examine their longer term options and to give them an incentive not to return to war. Similarly, in late 1995, virtually all of Mozambique's major donors—including the World Bank—took issue with the International Monetary Fund's (IMF's) demand that the Mozambique government make additional budget cuts to meet structural adjustment targets. In the view of the donors, additional fiscal restraint would run the risk of damaging Mozambique's development prospects, and they called instead for more investment.[21]

SCOPE OF ACTIVITIES

These constraints on emergency relief and development assistance constitute a strong argument in favor of creating a new category of assistance for countries emerging from civil wars. Assistance for the post-conflict transition phase should address three key needs of war-torn countries: strengthening political institutions, consolidating internal and external security, and inaugurating economic and social revitalization. (Box 8 summarizes the problems to be addressed by each of these objectives and the mechanisms available for doing so.) Clearly, many of these problems will not be resolved during the transition period. It is important, however, that they be tackled as early in the peacebuilding stage as possible. At a minimum, an awareness of these longer-term problems should inform actions to address the more immediate questions.

It is extremely difficult to rank areas to be addressed, although setting priorities is important. Two factors that strongly influence the order in which issues will be confronted are 1) the terms of the peace accords, and 2) the capacity of existing institutions and human resources.

During the transition phase, the emphasis is necessarily on implementing the peace accords. This often leaves little time and few resources for addressing activities not mandated by the accords but critical to the consolidation of peace. Of the peace accords surveyed for this essay, the Nicaraguan accords were the least comprehensive, covering only elections and demobilization of the Nicaraguan Resistance. The Salvadoran accords were the most complete, including vetting the officer corps for human rights violations, restructuring the police force, reforming and reducing the armed forces, demobilizing FMLN soldiers, reforming the electoral, legal, and judicial systems, establishing the FMLN as a political party, monitoring human rights practices, establishing a truth commission, and initiating reconstruction of the former conflict zones.

A related consideration is that there may be agreement that certain issues will not be dealt with until a new government has taken office. Under the terms of the Cambodian peace accords, "the main responsibility for deciding Cambodia's reconstruction needs and plans should rest with the Cambodian people and the government formed after free and fair elections."[22] Planning for reconstruction was thus unable to begin during the transition phase.

Although all war-torn countries have a weak base of institutional and human resources, some are better endowed than others. The genocidal policies of the Khmer Rouge left Cambodia with a deficit of human

BOX 8. POST-CONFLICT TRANSITION ASSISTANCE

OBJECTIVE

- Strengthen political institutions

PROBLEMS TO BE ADDRESSED

- Lack of government legitimacy
- Weak state incapable of fulfilling basic functions of government
- Overcentralization, resultant weakness of regional and local mechanisms
- Weak rule of law, significant human rights abuses
- Minimal experience with representative, participatory government
- Considerable disaffection with political leaders
- Poorly developed concept of "loyal opposition"
- Weak political parties; disintegrating wartime political coalitions
- Predominance of power politics; lack of consensus on national direction; insufficiently developed "rules of the game"; polarized society
- In situations with no clear winner, perception of all parties that their side has won, leading to an unrealistic assessment of political strength
- Absence of mechanisms to mediate intra-societal disputes
- Weak civil society organizations

MECHANISMS

- Strengthen electoral process
- Enact legal/judicial reforms to create system that provides for, inter alia, systematized dispute settlement, equality before the law for all
- Strengthen the legislature
- Strengthen public administration
- Institutionalize respect for human rights
- Identify the appropriate role for central government
- Strengthen local and regional governments
- Strengthen civil society
- Support truth commissions
- Undertake reconciliation efforts, both through specific programs and by infusing a spirit of reconciliation into all activities

BOX 8. POST-CONFLICT TRANSITION ASSISTANCE (continued)

OBJECTIVE

- Consolidate internal and external security

PROBLEMS TO BE ADDRESSED

- Bloated security establishment that must be reduced
- Armed opposition that must be disbanded/disarmed
- Armed forces control over internal security function
- Impunity
- Lack of public accountability of security forces
- Lack of civilian control over security forces
- Lack of mechanisms to evaluate true security needs
- Involvement of security force in political system and economy
- Lack of personal security for citizens

MECHANISMS

- Educate civilians in security-related issues
- Demobilize former combatants
- Disband paramilitary organizations
- End extra-legal forms of recruitment
- Redefine doctrine/missions of security forces
- Separate internal and external security functions
- Restructure security forces based on missions and budget
- Evaluate officers of former security forces (including armed opposition) prior to induction into new forces
- Reform the education of the military and police, stressing the role of security forces in democratic societies
- Institutionalize transparency and accountability
- Undertake reconciliation efforts, both through specific programs and by infusing the spirit of reconciliation into all activities
- Implement weapons buy-back schemes
- Undertake regional security initiatives

BOX 8. POST-CONFLICT TRANSITION ASSISTANCE (continued)

OBJECTIVE

- Promote economic and social revitalization

PROBLEMS TO BE ADDRESSED

- Extensive damage to economic and social infrastructure
- High level of debt
- Unsustainably high military budgets
- Landmines that hamper the resumption of economic activities
- Highly skewed distribution of income, wealth, and assets
- Multiple claims to land and assets
- Need to reintegrate severely war-affected populations (refugees, internally displaced persons, former combatants, child soldiers, disabled persons, women, orphans)
- Environmental degradation due to over-exploitation of natural resources, wartime movement of population, destruction of physical infrastructure
- Severely weakened social fabric (destruction of communities, creation of culture of violence, fostering a sense of impermanence and mistrust)
- Social disruptions created by the influx of returnees
- Abysmal indicators of human well-being

MECHANISMS

- Assess damage to economic and social infrastructure
- Provide technical assistance for rehabilitation and reconstruction
- Rehabilitate and reconstruct infrastructure
- Reactivate smallholder agriculture
- Rehabilitate export agriculture
- Rehabilitate key industries
- Undertake community revitalization
- Resettle the most severely war-affected groups
- Upgrade skills
- Generate employment, including credit, vocational training, management training, apprenticeships, microenterprise assistance
- Clear mines
- Strengthen local capacity to address problems
- Support regional economic initiatives

resources unparalleled in most other post-conflict states. Even with its record of flawed elections, El Salvador needed less electoral support than Cambodia and Mozambique, neither of which had ever held multiparty elections.

Despite these constraints, the experiences of recent peace processes suggest that the following activities should receive early attention even when they are not specified in the peace accords:

- Provide a sufficient level of internal security to enable economic activity to recover, to encourage refugees and internally displaced persons to reestablish themselves, and to persuade the business community to invest;
- Strengthen government's capacity to carry out key tasks;
- Assist the return of refugees and internally displaced persons;
- Support the rejuvenation of household economies, especially by strengthening the smallholder agriculture sector through the provision of inputs such as basic tools, seeds, and draft animals;
- Assist the recovery of communities, in part through projects that rehabilitate social and economic infrastructure;
- Rehabilitate economic infrastructure of crucial importance for economic revival;
- Remove land mines from major transport arteries, fields in heavily populated areas, and other critical sites;
- Stabilize the national currency and rehabilitate financial institutions;
- Promote national reconciliation; and
- Give priority to social groups and geographic areas most affected by the conflict.

DESIGN AND DELIVERY CHARACTERISTICS

If assistance for the post-conflict transition phase is to support the broad objectives of peacebuilding, special attention should be given to the design and delivery of donor programs. In post-conflict environments, there is a high premium on financial flexibility, contingency planning, sensitivity to local conditions, and conflict-resolution techniques and objectives.

FINANCIAL FLEXIBILITY. Financial flexibility is essential to the success of peacebuilding efforts. Although development practitioners time and again have stressed the importance of flexibility in the transition phase, their bureaucracies have not internalized this lesson fully.

Failure to deliver timely assistance can threaten the entire peace process. In El Salvador, the UNDP was forced to issue an emergency appeal for assistance to provision FMLN troops located in troop assembly areas shortly before cantonment was due to begin. USAID responded rapidly to this appeal because $35 million in counterpart funds generated by the P.L. 480 and Economic Support Fund programs was available for immediate disbursement as soon as the peace accords were signed.[23] Other donors were unable to respond until the demobilization process was nearly complete. Some U.N. officials feared that had there been inadequate accommodations for FMLN troops, the FMLN leadership might have broken off the demobilization process before it had even begun.

To speed the disbursement of post-conflict assistance for the transition phase, donors should adopt procedures similar to those governing the disbursement of emergency relief. One solution would be to create a stable but flexible source of financing that could be tapped for purposes related to the post-conflict transition. USAID has created such a source— the Office of Transition Initiatives—but the office's budget and staff are too small to enable it to tackle the problems to any meaningful extent. Given the general downsizing of development cooperation budgets, significant funds will probably not be earmarked for peacebuilding efforts in the future, with the possible exception of World Bank funds.[24]

It might, therefore, be more realistic to provide a "transition/ post-conflict waiver authority" to support peacebuilding activities. This should include waivers to restrictions on funding security forces that are contributing to the consolidation of peace. Most donors have constraints on funding militaries that can make it difficult, if not impossible, to finance crucial activities during the troop assembly phase of demobilization, and others have restrictions on assistance to police forces, which complicates the process of engaging in significant reform of the police.

Another possibility would be for donors to co-finance program loans with the multilateral development banks as a means of increasing the volume of quick-disbursing funds available to governments, as was done in El Salvador. Reprogramming is a frequently used option for speeding disbursement, but it presupposes the availability of significant funds, which is not always the case. At a minimum, all agencies involved in activities related to the peace process need to review their funding procedures with these issues in mind and to develop funding mechanisms that eliminate restrictive procedures and requirements as much as possible (see Box 9).[25]

CONTINGENCY PLANNING. The fluidity of peace processes puts a premium on contingency planning. It is impossible to predict the magni-

---

BOX 9. QUICK-DISBURSING FUNDS: LESSONS FROM EL SALVADOR

"A USAID [Mission] Must Have Access to Resources for at Least Humanitarian Activities Almost Immediately After the Cessation of Hostilities. These resources may be new USAID dollars, reprogrammed funds from existing projects, HCOLC [Host Country–Owned Local Currency], P.L. 480 Title II commodities, or a combination of the preceding. The requirements will be placed upon the mission quickly, and it will be expected to respond. The source(s) of the resources should provide the flexibility required to respond to a variety of needs. If USAID is looked to as the major donor by the USG [U.S. government], the host government and/or the U.N., it may come under pressure to fill gaps if other donors move slowly. Whatever USAID's role, USAID/Washington needs to be ready and able to respond rapidly to requests for flexible procurement procedures and to grant waivers as necessary and appropriate to avoid critical delays in implementation."

—USAID/El Salvador, "The First Three Years of the Peace and National Recovery Project (519-0394): Lessons Learned" (San Salvador: USAID, October 1994), p. 27.

"Although pledged donor support for the NRP [National Reconstruction Plan] has been generous, much of it has been in the form of slow-disbursing project financing, and most of it has not been directed at areas of highest political priority such as training and equipping the new national police, facilitating land transfers, etc. . . . The Government is . . . seeking cofinancing or parallel financing for SAL II in order to increase the volume of rapidly disbursing funds for NRP implementation."

—World Bank, "Report and Recommendation of the International Bank for Reconstruction and Development to the Executive Directors on the Proposed Second Structural Adjustment Loan (SAL) of US$50 Million to the Republic of El Salvador," report P-6108-ES (Washington, DC: World Bank, August 23, 1993), p. 5.

tude and nature of the problems that will arise as the peace accords are implemented during the transition phase, but even a cursory examination of recent peace processes illustrates that numerous obstacles will have to be surmounted. These hurdles include failure on the part of one or both parties to comply with key provisions of the accords, which may cause delays in implementation, changes in the composition or size of beneficiary pools, and demands for additional benefits that may be politically difficult to ignore (see Box 10).

Although events such as these are inevitable during the transition phase, contingency planning is not given the attention it warrants. Planners should ask "what if" at every stage of the process. In particular, they should anticipate delays in the implementation of politically sensitive provisions of the peace accords and give thought to the ways in which delays will affect each program.

SENSITIVITY TO LOCAL CONDITIONS. Understanding local needs and capacities is particularly critical in the politically charged post-conflict environment. Tailoring peacebuilding activities to local conditions requires overcoming special obstacles in post-conflict situations.

BOX 10. UNFORESEEN EVENTS IN MOZAMBIQUE

"A plan is an agreed-upon basis for change."

—ONUMOZ official, January 1995

■ It was initially assumed that the provisions of the Rome Accord, including presidential and legislative elections, would be implemented within a year of signing the agreement on October 4, 1992. Due to a variety of delays, the elections occurred on October 27–29, 1994.

■ A political agreement between the government and Renamo allowed an additional 16,000 government troops and members of the presidential guard to receive demobilization and reintegration benefits, increasing the beneficiary pool nearly 25 percent.

■ Troops that were to have been cantoned for six to eight weeks remained in camps up to six months pending resolution of political disagreements between the government and Renamo.

■ The ONUMOZ's Technical Unit for Demobilization planned to distribute a vegpack (consisting of vegetable seeds, a machete, and a bucket) only to former combatants returning to rural districts, but demobilized soldiers settling in urban areas demanded equal access to this benefit.

First, it can be difficult to obtain information about particular localities prior to the end of hostilities and in the early days of the peace process, when levels of mistrust are very high. Second, the post-conflict environment is extremely fluid, and information has to be updated continually. Third, it can also be difficult to obtain information about the intended beneficiaries of transition programs, such as former combatants, child soldiers, persons wounded in the war, and returnees. Finally, the speed with which programs have to be developed can also limit the ability to incorporate local input.

As is discussed in more detail below, donors can at least attempt to overcome these obstacles by becoming involved in the peace process during the negotiation phase. They could also base initial planning on strategies that have worked in similar circumstances or with similar types of beneficiaries. For example, vocational training programs for veterans could be viewed as a special form of adult basic education.[26] In addition, it is important to anticipate the need to incorporate innovative methods into program design. For example, training materials developed by the Occupational Skills Development program in Mozambique used either cartoons or pictures alone depending on the veterans' level of literacy. Learning by doing became an important pedagogical tool in an agricultural training program for former FMLN soldiers. As part of the program, veterans visited credit institutions and met with the staff who were going to process their credit applications. The institutions contracted to implement these training programs did not generally use such methods, and program staff had to help trainers to modify their methods.

Increased sensitivity to local conditions also requires that donors guard against assuming too much about target populations in the absence of detailed information about them or their environment. One assumption that frequently informs program design is that a person from a peasant background knows how to farm. If, however, that person left the family farm as a teenager and spent a decade in a refugee camp or in the armed forces, he or she is likely to need considerable assistance in becoming a productive farmer. The implementors of the agricultural training program for FMLN veterans, for example, found that "despite the *campesino* origins of the vast majority of the ex-combatants, many had little or no production experience previous to their integration into the FMLN guerrilla forces, in part due to the extreme youth of many of the ex-combatants."[27] In addition, it is important to consider whether farming constitutes a reasonable economic alternative for returnees given the prevailing economic environment.

To overcome this constraint, planners of peacebuilding programs constantly need to check their assumptions against existing conditions. To do so, donors and the agencies that implement peacebuilding programs should consult with a broad range of local actors so that their interventions make the maximum possible use of local knowledge and experience. At present, this rarely occurs.

According to repatriation expert Barry Stein, planners of refugee repatriation and reintegration efforts focus most of their attention on the refugees themselves and typically fail to give sufficient consideration to conditions in the country to which they will be repatriated. This refugee-oriented perspective may reflect the international community's attitude toward the country of origin—refugees often flee from repressive governments with which multilateral and bilateral governmental institutions have few direct contacts. But it also has its roots in bureaucratic politics. Relief operations place most of their resources in the country of asylum, since that is where refugees are located. These offices enjoy a higher status than offices in the country of origin and play a larger role in efforts to plan for repatriation and reintegration. This often leads to decisions concerning refugees that fail to take into account conditions in the country to which they will be repatriated and can have negative consequences for their subsequent involvement in productive activities and their social reintegration.

Finally, familiarity with local conditions is also hampered by the fact that some organizations only become active in a country once the war is over. For example, the World Bank often terminates lending operations as a result of conflicts and then finds itself in unfamiliar territory when it resumes lending after the fighting stops. Many NGOs that act as implementing agencies for donors have no experience in the countries to which they send staff. Some have never worked in a post-conflict environment. For example, a number of the organizations that became involved in rehabilitating Rwanda following the 1994 genocide had never worked in a developing country, and the vast majority had never worked in an emergency environment.

Organizations that are not familiar with conditions on the ground can develop programs and pursue policies that hamper reconciliation, thereby endangering a fragile peace. Donor agencies need to ensure that both their own staff and that of agencies executing their programs are knowledgeable about the conflict and its effect on society, the economy, and the political system, so that they can understand the ramifications of their actions.

External actors can take several steps to minimize their potential to disrupt the peace process. First, organizations that have no recent experience with the country in question should gain access to current information—in the form of briefing papers, via the Internet, and so on—prior to their arrival. Once established in the country, expatriate employees should receive detailed briefings on the conflict and its consequences. Where feasible, linking international NGOs with local NGOs could improve the knowledge that external agencies have of the local environment.[28]

INCORPORATING CONFLICT RESOLUTION TECHNIQUES AND OBJECTIVES. Peace accords are most often concluded after lengthy negotiations, yet the negotiating process rarely, if ever, ends when the accords are signed. First of all, peace agreements are often silent on critical issues that invariably surface early on in the transition phase, and reaching an agreement on how to deal with them must be accorded high priority.

Second, although peace treaties specify *what* is to occur, they typically do not say *how* it will occur. The parties to the conflict frequently disagree on how to implement the agreements and may have unrealistic expectations both about their relative political strength and about the amount of assistance the donors will make available for peacebuilding. Third, unforeseen questions and unanticipated consequences arise that must be dealt with. Furthermore, the need for conflict-resolution mechanisms may be especially acute during the period immediately following signing of the agreements.

In consequence, two critical post-conflict requirements for donors are: 1) establishing mechanisms for resolving issues that arise during the implementation phase, and 2) helping the parties to move from negotiation to dialogue intended to reach consensus on how to solve specific problems.

Peace accords frequently establish commissions to assist in the implementation process. In some cases, as in Mozambique, the commissions are constituted as decision-making bodies. In others, such as El Salvador, they function as monitors. (See Box 11.) Irrespective of their legal status, formal commissions rarely function as envisioned by the accords because of political divisions between the parties.

External actors can help these commissions to approach issues as problems to solve rather than as political opportunities. In many cases, the diplomatic community is charged with supervising these commissions.

BOX 11. COMMISSIONS GUIDING THE PEACE PROCESS IN MOZAMBIQUE

The General Peace Agreement created seven commissions to implement its provisions. The main commission was the Supervisory and Monitoring Commission (CSC), composed of representatives of the government, Renamo, the United Nations, the Organization of African Unity, and other invited parties. It was chaired by the United Nations. Three subsidiary commissions were the Joint Commission for the Formation of the Mozambican Defense Force (CCFADM), the Cease-Fire Commission (CCF), and the Reintegration Commission (CORE). The structure of CORE and the CCF were similar to that of the CSC. CCFADM did not have a U.N. chair. Three additional commissions were the Police Commission, the Intelligence Commission, and the Joint Commission for Territorial Administration.

Members of CORE believed that they learned to work well with one another. In general, however, the commissions did not function satisfactorily. The driving force behind the successful implementation of the accords was the special representative of the secretary-general who prodded the two parties into compliance with the active support of the diplomatic community in Maputo.

In part, the relatively more productive environment within CORE derived from personal relations between government and Renamo representatives that existed before the conflict. The creation of a technical working group to evaluate proposals and reach agreements that were then presented to the parties' senior CORE representatives for final approval at the political level was also helpful. Problems sometimes arose, however, because the government's technical and political tracks were poorly coordinated, while any agreement that Renamo accepted at the technical level had already been vetted by the political leadership. The U.N. Office for Humanitarian Assistance Coordination chaired CORE meetings, and representatives of the donor community were also actively involved.

In some cases, such as the Commission on Reintegration in Mozambique, which was responsible for reintegrating former combatants, donor representatives play this role. All external personnel who participate in the work of formal commissions should receive training in conflict resolution and consensus-building techniques. Some donors seem to have learned this lesson, but few appear to have acted on it.[29]

The technical working group has been employed frequently to develop consensus among the former parties to the conflict (see Box 12). Technical working groups are formed to accomplish a specific task. In El Salvador, for example, technical working groups were created to address discrete problems facing demobilized FMLN soldiers, such as assistance to the disabled, credit, land tenancy, and housing. Similarly, two working groups were established to facilitate the implementation of UNDP's integrated agricultural training program for demobilized FMLN troops. The first dealt with political issues, including the level of financial and food subsidies for trainees and eligibility criteria for program participants; the second dealt with technical issues, primarily the structure and content of the training courses themselves.[30]

Technical working groups require the active participation of donor representatives who not only are trained in the techniques of conflict resolution and consensus building but also can design programs that promote reconciliation and consensus.[31] In addition, in forming these groups it is important to take account of wartime relationships between donors

---

BOX 12. GENERATING WIN-WIN OUTCOMES

One important lesson that USAID extracted from the peace process in El Salvador was that when working with the parties to implement programs related to the peace accords, meetings should be

"tripartite, i.e., both belligerent sides—depending on the situation in a country, one side may be both the government and its military— and the USAID mission. They should be participatory and problem-solving in nature with the objective of reaching win-win solutions. The USAID mission should make every effort to be—and to be seen as—an honest broker interested only in efficient and effective interventions."

Source: USAID/El Salvador, "The First Three Years of the Peace and National Recovery Project (519-0394): Lessons Learned" (San Salvador: USAID, October 1994), p. 25.

and the parties to the conflict. As a general principle, a lead agency should be designated for a specific task only if both sides of the conflict have been consulted. Parties should be given the opportunity to determine what the working relationship with donor representatives will be if the donor's government strongly supported any of the parties during the conflict.

ESTABLISHING A NEW POLITICAL CULTURE. To be effective, conflict resolution and consensus building should not be limited to specific programs or processes associated with implementing the peace accords. Ideally, they should inform all interactions among citizens and between citizens and the state. Compromise must replace violent conflict as the means of resolving differences among social groups (see Box 13).

Collaborative modes of behavior need to be fostered. Designing projects so that different groups have an incentive to cooperate and changing how language is used are two methods of furthering this objective. For example, Salvadoran NGOs that were FMLN supporters in wartime complained during the transition phase that USAID staff still referred to them as FMLN NGOs, although they did not label NGOs associated with the Arena party or the Christian Democratic party (PDC) as Arena NGOs or PDC NGOs. An external evaluation of USAID's programs recommended classifying NGOs according to the area of expertise, geographic location, or administrative and financial management capacity but "not by the politics of its board of directors."[32]

BOX 13. BUILDING A CULTURE OF PEACE

"For the vast majority of this century, we have been living in a culture of war. The transition from a culture of war to a culture of peace calls for a new approach to conflict. Building a culture of peace involves changing attitudes, beliefs, and behaviours—from everyday life situations to high-level negotiations between countries—so that our natural response to conflict would be nonviolent and our instinctive reactions would be toward negotiation and reason, not aggression."

—UNESCO, "First Consultative Meeting of the Culture of Peace Program, Paris September 27–29, 1994. Final Report," CPP-94/ CONF.601/3 (Paris: UNESCO, October 14, 1994), p. 2.

Collaboration can be cultivated by guaranteeing all relevant groups—from the local to the national level—a seat at the table when issues of importance to them are being discussed. During the transition phase, the parties to the conflict are often consumed by the political infighting that accompanies the dissolution of wartime coalitions and are consequently unable to represent adequately the interests of ordinary citizens, particularly those who have been most affected by the war.[33] Supporting the empowerment of civil society can help to mitigate the detrimental effects of this behavior by offering citizens the means to make their voices heard, especially at the local level.

. . . .

MAXIMIZING THE RETURNS ON INVESTMENT IN THE TRANSITION PHASE

"It is now recognized that implementation of the settlement in the time prescribed may not be enough to guarantee that the conflict will not revive. Coordinated programmes are required, over a number of years and in various fields, to ensure that the original causes of the war are eradicated."

—U.N. General Assembly/Security Council, *Supplement to an Agenda for Peace: Position Paper of the Secretary-General on the Occasion of the Fiftieth Anniversary of the United Nations*[34]

■ THERE HAS BEEN A TENDENCY TO ASSUME that diplomatic and military efforts should be concentrated in the negotiation, cessation of hostilities, and transition phases, while financial and technical assistance should be concentrated in the transition phase.[35] In fact, the entire range of institutions that constitute the international community has a role to play in all phases of the peace process.

Because of the profound mistrust and animosity generated by civil wars, the extreme institutional weaknesses characteristic of post-conflict countries, and the destruction visited on society and the economy by armed conflict, repairing the ravages of war is an arduous, complex, and lengthy process. For countries moving simultaneously from highly exclusionary political systems to more open and participatory forms of government and from centralized economic systems to economies responsive to market forces, the process is even more complicated. It is unrealistic to expect that peace in these countries will be consolidated in less than a generation. What is more, it is by no means inevitable that, once set in motion, the peace process will succeed. It is therefore crucial that the international community strongly support conflict resolution and sustain its assistance throughout the peacebuilding phase.

At first glance, this time frame would appear to create substantial problems for the donors. The typical donor's time horizon is years, not decades, and donors need to justify continued funding by regularly demonstrating progress toward a specific objective. However, because the peace process is composed of distinct phases, each consisting of numerous discrete activities, it is not difficult to combine a long-term commitment with a step-by-step—or program-by-program—approach. What is needed is the political will to make that long-term commitment.

Once a commitment to support the peace process is made in principle, donors should maintain the maximum flexibility in how they define the programs they will support. Based on its institutional comparative advantage, in discussion with the broadest possible range of local actors, and in close coordination with other members of the international development community, each donor should devise a long-term plan for building peace. This plan would define the overall objectives of the assistance to be provided and outline the major programs that might be implemented to support these goals. It should not, however, commit donors to funding and implementing every component of the master plan. Options should be kept open for at least three reasons. First, funding will be approved incrementally. Second, it is impossible to foresee precisely how needs will unfold over any given period of time. Third, host governments should not view programs as an entitlement, because the initial plan may change for any number of reasons.

This approach requires closely monitoring each component of the long-term plan. Each program that is implemented should receive a mid-term evaluation that determines whether it is feasible and desirable to move on to the next program envisioned in the plan. If the answer is yes, then preparations for the next step should begin immediately. The success of this strategy depends to a large degree on giving program managers in the field adequate freedom and initiative to adjust both ongoing programs and the plans for follow-on programs.

The degree and nature of donor involvement required vary from phase to phase. During negotiations, a relatively modest amount of resources should be devoted to planning and to building collaborative relationships with the parties to the conflict. During the cessation of hostilities, donors should begin matching assumptions made during planning with realities on the ground and finalizing programs that need to begin early in the transition phase. Donors involved in demobilization may need to provide assistance at this point to begin equipping troop assembly areas. The focus during the transition phase is on assisting the parties to comply with the terms of the peace agreements. It is in this phase that the heaviest demands are made on donor resources. During the consolidation phase, post-conflict countries primarily need assistance in maintaining the gains achieved and in deepening the reform of political institutions and the security sector. Although recent experience suggests that the level of assistance may decrease at the end of the transition phase, a significant decline will reduce the leverage exercised by donors.

The following sections examine in more detail the contributions that the donors can make to the peace process in the two major phases that precede and follow the transition phase: the negotiation and consolidation phases.

THE NEGOTIATION PHASE

To date, the voice of the development community has been weak or nonexistent at most negotiating tables. Negotiations are essentially a political undertaking, with responsibility lodged in international and regional political bodies and the foreign and defense ministries of interested states. There is, nonetheless, considerable scope for donor agencies to play a supporting role during the negotiation phase.

THE CASE FOR DONOR INVOLVEMENT. There are several reasons why the donors should play a larger role during the negotiation process than they have previously: 1) to ensure that relevant economic issues are put on the negotiating table in a realistic manner; 2) to develop mechanisms for solving crucial economic issues that are likely to become politicized or ignored once the peace agreement is signed; 3) to avoid raising unrealistic expectations about the amount and nature of donor assistance that will be available to support the peace process; 4) to encourage advance planning by the donors; 5) to offer the parties tangible benefits on signature of the accords; and 6) to begin to build close working relationships with the parties to the conflict and other groups in society to facilitate implementation of the peace accords.

Although they may have been critical to the genesis of armed conflict, economic factors are rarely taken into account during peace negotiations. As a result, few peace agreements have addressed the economic causes of the conflict in the same measure as they address the political and security causes. Where the peace agreement has included provisions relating to economic and social issues, those provisions have not sufficiently taken local conditions into account. For example, the El Salvador peace agreement stipulated that land tenure conflicts were to be settled within six months of the signing of the cease-fire agreement. This time frame was established although the procedure for transferring title was extremely complex, the 1980s land transfer programs had taken a decade to complete, and the process of identifying beneficiaries was not likely to be straightforward. If development specialists had been consulted during the negotiation phase, it might have been possible to devise a set of measures that would have compensated FMLN supporters over a more realistic period of time. Alternatively, if agreement on specific measures could not be reached, it might have been possible to agree on the principle of compensation and the establishment of a joint government-FMLN mechanism, perhaps chaired by the United Nations, to iron out the details once the peace accords came into effect.

Donors should be included in the negotiating process to minimize the possibility that parties will be promised more than can be delivered. Expectations are typically very high in post-conflict countries. Years of war-induced deprivation have come to an end, and the population wants their lives to change as rapidly as possible. It is therefore crucial to be as realistic as possible about the nature and volume of assistance that should be anticipated. Consulting with donors during the negotiating process will not eliminate this problem entirely, but sending a clear signal about the probable level of funding is an important step toward minimizing the tendency to make excessive promises. For example, Guatemala's major donors have sought to impress upon the government that "the primary responsibility [for financing the peace accords] will fall to Guatemala."[36]

Involving donors early in the process enhances the opportunities for advance planning, which has been absent in many peace processes to date, especially outside the realm of economic reconstruction (see Box 14). If they were closely involved in the negotiating process, donors would have sufficient time to include funding requests for peacebuilding programs in their regular budgets and would not be forced to launch emergency appeals. There would be more opportunity for coordination, and more thought could be given to program design. More active involvement by the international development community at this point might also increase the donors' commitment to support all elements of the peace accords. At present, some programs—such as police reform and assistance to soldiers awaiting demobilization—appear to hold a low priority for many donors. Finally, peacebuilding assistance could be used to induce the parties to reach agreement.

An additional argument in favor of inaugurating the planning process during the final stages of the negotiation phase is that once under way, peace processes develop a momentum that makes it difficult to see beyond the short term. Issues that are not of immediate concern tend to be put on the back burner, where they often stay until just before programs are implemented, at which point it is realized that planning has

---

BOX 14. ADVANCE PLANNING BY USAID/EL SALVADOR

"As the peace process began to accelerate in early 1991, the USAID mission began to explore what it could do to support the national reconstruction program being elaborated by the GOES [Government of El Salvador] and the process of national reconciliation and economic stabilization that would need to follow the termination of the conflict.

"This led to two actions: a) the pre-positioning of 100 million colones ($13.5 million equivalent at that time) of Host Country–Owned Local Currency which would be available for immediate disbursement by the GOES upon signature of the Peace Accords; and b) the development of a Project Paper for the Peace and National Recovery Project (519-0394)."

—USAID/El Salvador, "The First Three Years of the Peace and National Recovery Project (519-0394): Lessons Learned" (San Salvador: USAID, October 1994), pp. 7–8.

not been sufficient. For example, planning for the reinsertion and reintegration of former combatants is typically postponed because attention is focused on cantonment and demobilization. These programs that aim to reintroduce the military into civilian life cannot, however, be put in place rapidly. A joint mission to Angola by USAID and the U.S. State Department in December 1994 concluded that a six- to nine-month planning period is needed.[37]

Early planning is constrained by the lack of information about a variety of crucial issues: conditions in the areas where fighting has occurred, the specific needs of beneficiaries in these regions (including the armed opposition), the speed with which refugees and displaced persons will return home, and so on. This means that any plans developed before the accords are signed should be reviewed by all parties before final approval of program design and project implementation.

Last, but by no means least, during the negotiation phase donors should aim to improve the level of trust between them and the parties to the conflict and perhaps even between the parties themselves. Donors should also seek to establish working relations with close allies of the parties. Building such relationships could improve access of donors to certain beneficiary groups and geographic regions and speed implementation during the transition phase. It could also enable the donors to press the parties to address key economic and social imbalances that were not dealt with in the peace accords but must be confronted for consolidation of a lasting peace.

MECHANISMS FOR DONOR INVOLVEMENT. There are several ways in which an economic and developmental perspective can be injected into the peace process at an early stage. The least formal mechanism would be for the mediators to consult with representatives of the donor community on an informal basis. World Bank and U.N. agency representatives have been consulted during the Guatemalan peace process in this way.

A more formal and as yet untried approach would be to create a technical advisory committee composed of representatives of the country's major multilateral and bilateral development partners. This committee would provide mediators and parties to the conflict with information on subjects related to the economy and to development in much the way that military officers from selected countries provide information on the technical aspects of cease-fire, separation of forces, and so on.

This group could review the relevant provisions of the accords to evaluate whether they can be implemented, whether the proposed implementation schedule is appropriate, and whether funding is likely to be available. It could also suggest alternative approaches that might help to overcome obstacles in the negotiating process. Finally, it could provide a conduit for input from groups other than the parties to the conflict. This might increase the legitimacy of such groups in the eyes of the parties and might foster consultation between the parties and civil society.

An additional mechanism that would complement formal or informal advisory groups is working groups in which the parties, preferably jointly but independently at first if necessary, could discuss technical issues with donors before the accords are signed. These working groups could start the parties on the path to reconciliation and signal the beginning of a working relationship between the parties and major supporters of the peace process. Such a process would place on the table the expectations of the signatories and the technical and financial feasibility of various types of interventions. Ultimately, this should facilitate implementation. Again, donors could use this opportunity to interject proposals from other segments of society into the discussion.

THE CONSOLIDATION PHASE

Although the installation of an elected government signals that the transition phase has ended, it does not indicate that all provisions of the peace accords have been implemented. In some instances, compliance has been incomplete because one or more of the parties has knowingly failed to meet its obligations on schedule. In El Salvador, for example, government inaction delayed implementation of the land transfer program and the establishment of the National Civil Police.[38] In Cambodia, none of the four armed groups met its demobilization target. However, not all of peace agreement provisions can be fully realized in one or two years, which is generally the time allotted between the signing of accords and the holding of elections. Even if creation of the National Civil Police had not been obstructed, establishing a new police force would have taken at least four years, and El Salvador would still have required international assistance after the March 1994 elections.

Therefore, a first priority of the donors and other members of the international community during the consolidation phase must be to work with the parties to ensure compliance with the accords. This involves funding relevant programs initiated during the transition phase and pressuring the parties to take any steps necessary to meet obligations incurred under the peace agreement. Donors may have to withhold or threaten to withhold aid to encourage one or all parties to comply. Such conditionality should, however, be distinguished from withholding assistance for partisan purposes, such as has been the case with U.S. assistance to Nicaragua since the early 1990s.

The capacity of donors to apply pressure may be limited in some cases, as it was when the Khmer Rouge refused to demobilize its troops. In these instances, the international diplomatic community has a responsibility to enforce compliance. To accomplish this, it may be desirable to extend the mandate of the peacekeeping operation, as was done on several occasions with the U.N. Observer Mission in El Salvador (ONUSAL).[39] Some problems, such as the refusal of the Khmer Rouge to demobilize, may not be amenable to solution under the existing mandate of the peacekeeping operation, and unless the member states of the organizations charged with carrying out peacekeeping missions are willing to expand that mandate, the international community has little leverage.

For the most part, attention shifts during the second phase of peacebuilding to activities not specifically required by the peace agreement but nonetheless critical for consolidating the peace. These are primarily the activities that strengthen institutions; reform the civil service, security sector, and legal system; and develop the legislature and political party system. Also included are measures to correct economic and social imbalances.

At this stage, donors should focus on building capacity in both the governmental and nongovernmental sectors, which means transferring essential knowledge and skills. In view of the extreme institutional weakness of post-conflict societies, donors have tended to provide foreign experts who fulfill critical gaps without necessarily transferring their skills and knowledge to local personnel. Officials of governmental and other organizations have to develop the capacity to perform critical tasks on their own. The donor community is well aware of this need, and some donors are taking measures to ensure that it is met. Donors need to make the transfer of knowledge and skills a top priority (see Box 15).

Finally, an additional objective of strengthening nongovernmental actors should be to expand the capacity of civil society to monitor programs and analyze their policy implications. Few NGOs in war-torn societies have the capacity to conduct rigorous policy analysis. As a result, they tend to react to events and are primarily confrontational in their responses to government policies at a time when there is great need for balanced analyses.

Donors can support the objectives of the consolidation phase through their bilateral programs, through multilateral programs overseen by U.N. agencies or multilateral development banks, and through efforts

BOX 15. TECHNICAL ASSISTANCE TO MOZAMBIQUE

"We agree, as the UNDP coordinator reminded us, that we the donor community must continue thinking or rather re-thinking the most appropriate forms of technical assistance, of which there may well be an excess supply and which is certainly not used in an optimal fashion. We must learn to ration this super-abundant good in a way that best serves the interests of the recipient, not just those of some of our bureaucracies, whether bilateral or multilateral."[a]

—"Chair's Closing Statement," Mozambique Consultative Group Meeting, Paris, March 14-15, 1995.

"Regarding aid modalities we would like to comment [on] the use of technical assistance. Sweden has over the last few years been engaged in a process of phasing out the previously large component of technical assistance in the form of individual contracts with gap-filling persons.

"At present we have technical assistance in two principal forms:
■ The first is the personnel fund, where Sweden makes available annual amounts that the Mozambican government can utilize for hiring of expatriate staff as it sees fit.
■ The second form is the provision of personnel for capacity- and institution-building functions within well-defined sector programmes, where transfer of knowledge is guaranteed through back-stopping services from institutions in outside countries."[b]

—"Swedish Bilateral Assistance to Mozambique: Pledging Statement," Mozambique Consultative Group Meeting, Paris, March 14–15, 1995.

to ensure that Consultative Group and Round Table meetings continue to address key issues. Most of the institutional objectives of this phase of peacebuilding would have a high priority even if the country were not moving from war to peace. With one exception, they represent issues that development assistance has traditionally addressed over the last 40 years and that have, in recent years, received considerable attention. That one exception is reform of the security sector. Although many countries would benefit from reform of their security apparatus, donor interest in pressing for change has been limited for the most part. However, the need for such reform is particularly urgent in post-conflict countries.

. . . .

REFORMING INTERNAL AND EXTERNAL SECURITY STRUCTURES

"One of the priorities of the programme for modernization of the Salvadoran State, established pursuant to the peace accords, concerns the demilitarization of the public security apparatus and the development and application of a new doctrine. . . . In recent months, a number of situations have arisen which could affect this process: principally, these involve the deployment of the army in rural areas to perform public security functions and the announcement of a possible extension of this deployment to some cities; reports of human rights violations by agents of the new police force; the delay in appointing supervisory personnel as well as the appointment of personnel with questionable credentials to certain posts; and the absence of legal measures applicable to the operation of the public security apparatus as a whole."

—U.N. General Assembly, *Strengthening the Coordination of Humanitarian and Disaster Relief of the United Nations, Including Special Economic Assistance: Special Economic Assistance to Individual Countries or Regions: Assistance for the Reconstruction and Development of El Salvador*[40]

THE REFORM AGENDA

To consolidate the peace and prevent the recurrence of conflict, fundamental reforms must be carried out in the security sector. Some reform of the security sector is generally mandated by the peace agreements. Peace agreements typically require government forces to be reduced and armed opposition forces to be dismantled. The accords may also dictate restructuring the armed forces to merge the forces of the government with those of the opposition, reorienting the mission of the armed forces from internal to external security, reforming the police force, dismantling paramilitary forces, and subordinating all security forces to civilian authorities.[41]

Peace agreements are often silent or vague about how these changes are to occur. They rarely address underlying conditions that seriously complicate efforts to undertake reform—for example, the absence of civilian institutions to supervise and monitor the security sector, the lack of transparency on the entire range of issues pertaining to security, and the lack of civilian personnel knowledgeable in security issues. In consequence, post-conflict countries should seek to deepen the reform process initiated by the peace accords.

As a first step, governments should clearly separate internal and external security functions, assigning responsibility for guaranteeing external security to the armed forces and responsibility for maintaining domestic law and order to the civilian police force. The police and the military should become separate institutions, and both should be under civilian control. The ministry of defense should be staffed by civilians, at least some of whom have not served in the armed forces.

The creation of a civilian police force that protects, rather than preys on, the ordinary citizen is essential. In the past—for example, in El Salvador and Haiti—members of the old police force or even of the armed forces have been allowed to participate in the new force following a vetting process. This path has been chosen in no small measure because of the difficulties in constructing a civilian police force from the ground up, particularly in a post-conflict environment where there are many immediate threats to law and order which must not be ignored. There is, however, a growing body of evidence suggests that retaining even a small number of officers from the old, corrupted force is counterproductive.[42]

Second, governments should institutionalize mechanisms for conducting formal, realistic assessments of their security needs. The size and structure of the forces should be determined by the country's security environment, the available resources, and the feasibility of guaranteeing external security using nonmilitary methods, such as participation in regional security fora and regional security agreements.

Third, there should be greater transparency within the security forces, the executive branch, and the legislature on security-related issues. In virtually all post-conflict countries, security matters have traditionally been shrouded in secrecy. Decisions have been made by a small number of policymakers, most often within the military establishment, and very little information about levels of expenditure, size and composition of forces, or equipment procured has been made public, even to the ministry of finance and the legislature. While there is clearly a need for confidentiality in some areas, withholding basic information about the military sector serves no purpose other than to protect the security sector from public scrutiny. Rather than promoting security, secrecy frequently leads to the misallocation of resources, undermining a country's economic stability. The military has the responsibility to provide input into the planning and budgeting processes, but final decisions about the level of forces, equipment, and budgets are properly the domain of civilians in the executive and legislative branches of government.

Fourth, the training of civilian security analysts should have high priority. In countries where the military has played a central role in politics for many years, the military usually firmly believes that civilians are incapable of evaluating security requirements. Most post-conflict countries have a paucity of civilian security analysts, both inside and outside government, but capability is not the primary issue. Rather, the shortage of civilian security analysts derives in large part from the military's unwillingness to share information with civilians. However, until a cadre of security specialists exists, it will be difficult to demonstrate that there is a viable alternative to the military's monopoly over this sector.

Fifth, the government needs to make the political decision that all security-related expenditures and revenues will be placed on budget and that the armed forces will no longer be allowed to own and operate businesses and otherwise engage in economic activities. Finally, channels need to be created for civilian-military dialogue, involving not only civilian government officials but also members of private sector organizations. Such dialogue will build confidence and improve the ability of civilians to analyze defense issues.

Some of these reforms can be put in place more rapidly than others, such as establishing channels for civilian-military dialogue and placing all security-related expenditures and revenue on budget. All will require the government's sustained attention over a period of years. It is therefore important that they are addressed as early as possible.

ROLE OF THE DONOR COMMUNITY

Although the primary responsibility for reforming the security sector rests with the governments of war-torn countries, the donor community can facilitate the process by providing advice, technical assistance, and funding and by applying pressure as necessary. To be fully effective in this area, the donors will need to collaborate with other members of the international community, such as representatives of foreign and defense ministries, civilian law enforcement agencies, and the armed forces of interested countries, as well as regional organizations and NGOs. The donor interventions needed during the different phases of the peace process are outlined below.

NEGOTIATION AND CESSATION OF HOSTILITIES PHASES. Donors should undertake two main activities during these phases. Ideally these efforts should be aimed at both the government and the armed opposition. The latter is frequently wary of becoming involved in security-related issues at this stage, but its early participation will facilitate subsequent implementation of the peace accords. Technical advisory committees and working groups are the most suitable formats for these interactions.

First, donors can inform the parties about the type of assistance they can expect during implementation of particular provisions of the accords, such as demobilization of forces, reintegration of demobilized troops, and separation of external security and civilian policing functions. They can also indicate the amount of assistance likely to be forthcoming. Knowing what assistance will be available could encourage the parties to conclude the negotiations and help to manage expectations, which are frequently unrealistically high with regard to reintegration programs. In particular, if long-term reintegration assistance for veterans is to be combined with programs aimed at other returnees and vulnerable groups rather than targeted solely to the veterans themselves, the reasons for this decision should be explained at this point.

Second, donors can begin to build relations with the parties that will facilitate the rapid implementation of programs to assist former combatants. One of the problems confronting the persons who plan demobilization and especially reintegration programs is their lack of information about the troops to be demobilized. Having the information to develop generic profiles and learn more about the needs of soldiers early in the process would facilitate the ability of decision makers to plan, but this information is rarely forthcoming because the parties suspect that it might be used against them.[43] Bringing the parties together to discuss technical issues could create a climate of mutual trust that would speed implementation.

Finally, as soon as the peace agreement is signed, donors may need to provide financial and technical support for troop assembly areas in preparation for demobilization.

TRANSITION PHASE. During the transition phase, the focus is first and foremost on compliance with the provisions of the peace accords. For the donors, this generally means supporting soldiers in cantonment areas awaiting demobilization. It may also involve assisting with the creation or strengthening of civilian police forces and providing assistance to bodies vetting members of the security forces for past human rights abuses. If a new security force is to be created, it is worth exploring whether the officers can receive early training in their role according to the constitution, the principles and mechanisms of democratic civil-military relations, and international law on armed conflict and human rights. However, as long as the transition phase lasts only a year or two, it is unlikely that elements of the reform agenda that are not expressly included in the accords will be addressed at this point.

CONSOLIDATION PHASE. Once into the consolidation phase, donors can work with other members of the international community to promote thorough reform of the security sector.

First, donors can provide governments with technical assistance to develop good budgeting practices in the security sector. This involves ensuring that the budgets of the security forces are detailed, that all expenditures related to security are clearly identified irrespective of their place in the budget, and that all expenditures of the security forces are placed on the budget and all security sector revenues are identified. In addition, the security budget must be made available to members of the legislature in a timely fashion so that they can review and debate its contents before voting on the national budget. To facilitate this process and build institutional capacity as required, donors could provide technical assistance, in the form of independent consultants, to help governments to develop the capacity to assess their long-term strategic environment. Where feasible, such consultants should come from the region, rather than from donor countries.

Second, donors can provide scholarships to civilians, both government officials and members of civil society, for training in security studies, defense budgeting and management, and other relevant subjects. It is particularly important to train nongovernmental analysts, both to create a pool of specialists that governments can draw on subsequently and to enhance civil society's capacity to monitor government policies and actions.

Third, in collaboration with other members of the international community, donors can create channels for civilian-military dialogue. One example of such assistance would be to finance meetings in a variety of venues at which civilians and members of the military would share their perspectives on issues related to security. Another would be to include both civilian and military officials in relevant discussions between donors and the government.

A fourth area in which donors can promote security sector reform is the civilianization of police forces. Here, donors can support professional training for both the armed forces and the police force to strengthen the application of the rule of law and the protection of human rights. Funds could be created to support this training, such as the European Union fund for improving the observance of human rights in Central America. Alternatively, training could be conducted through the military education system.

Finally, donors can assist governments in gaining control over enterprises run by the military and determining whether these enterprises should be under public or private ownership. Where it is agreed that these enterprises should not be state-owned, donors can assist governments in privatizing them.[44] In addition to reducing the scope for independent action on the part of the armed forces, "civilianizing" military-owned enterprises will strengthen the military budgeting process by reducing off-budget expenditures.

Consultative Groups and Round Tables have an important role to play in seeing the reform process through to its conclusion. They can ensure that key issues are on the agenda and that specific steps are discussed at each meeting. As a group, member countries of the OECD's Development Assistance Committee have already begun to consider how they might help to redress imbalances between civilians and the military in economic and political affairs. Possible actions include engendering dialogue on the roles of each group, developing civilian expertise in defense budgeting, and providing advice on reducing military expenditures, including demobilization and reintegration of former combatants.[45]

Regrettably, although Consultative Groups and similar fora have raised the question of imbalances between security expenditures and other budgetary categories, such as social services, they have generally not discussed specific actions that government can take to reform the security sector. It would be extremely helpful if donors would discuss specific steps that government should be taking, in much the way that the March 1995 Consultative Group meeting for Mozambique reviewed the country's democratic reforms. This meeting examined specific objectives relating to the operation of the National Assembly, the role of the opposition and a free press, decentralization and civil society, good governance, and the development of an independent judiciary. The government was commended for taking certain steps to achieve these goals, and the donors noted instances where they hoped to see additional progress.[46] Discussions of this nature should be complemented by offers of financial and technical support to meet agreed-upon objectives where feasible.

Resident aid missions in war-torn countries should keep the subject of security sector reform before the government. In this regard, aid missions should work closely with the diplomatic community, including military attachés. Attention has been given to initiating civil-military dialogue and discussing the role of the security forces in democratic societies. These areas are, in a sense, the easiest to address, since they primarily involve holding meetings. More emphasis needs to be placed on building the institutional capacity for good governance in the security sector.

Finally, the resident diplomatic community should devise a method for monitoring the activities and the role of the security forces following the termination of peacekeeping missions. Disbursement of development assistance could be linked to compliance on key issues. This assumes, however, that the level of aid remains sufficiently high to leverage the government.

· ·

THE POLITICS OF PEACEBUILDING

"A USAID [mission] probably will be faced with project counterparts and beneficiaries holding deep-seated emotions, and mutual distrust and animosities towards each other—and perhaps toward the USAID [mission] if it is identified with one side of the conflict—due to their recent belligerent status. And there may be a number of political agendas being pushed. There must be strong consideration of the political dimension of the project and a good understanding of the political forces at play."

—USAID/El Salvador, "The First Three Years of the Peace and National Recovery Project (519-0394): Lessons Learned"[47]

■ BECAUSE PEACEBUILDING ACTIVITIES are inherently political and are implemented in highly politicized situations, the selection, design, and implementation of programs cannot be approached from a purely technical point of view. Political considerations can both improve and weaken program quality, and the international donor community should work to minimize the negative effects and maximize the positive ones. Donors often lack the political weight necessary to encourage the parties to adopt a particular course of action and need to be backed by sustained diplomatic support.

RELATIONS BETWEEN DONORS AND THE PARTIES TO THE CONFLICT

The policies of bilateral donor governments during wartime inevitably color the relations between their aid agencies and parties to the conflict during the peace process. Bilateral aid agencies need to analyze how the new political environment affects their operations. Multilateral agencies should also undertake such a review, because their presence in or absence from the country during the conflict will influence their relations with the parties. The experience of USAID in El Salvador illustrates how failure to reconsider wartime relationships can create a situation in which opportunities are missed both to develop technically sound programs and to create an environment more conducive to collaboration between the parties.

The United States was a major player in the civil war in El Salvador, and its relationship with Salvadoran government agencies was very close. The National Secretariat for Reconstruction (SRN), which has been the government's primary conduit for assistance mandated under the peace accords to the most war-affected zones, had its origins in the National Commission for the Restoration of Areas, the agency that implemented the government's U.S.-backed economic counterinsurgency strategy. USAID/El Salvador decided to make the SRN the main vehicle for distributing U.S. aid to the peace process. One of the justifications for this choice was that use of the SRN would promote reconciliation "by forcing the FMLN to deal with the GOES [Government of El Salvador], as opposed to having USAID deal with the FMLN." Unfortunately, although the FMLN and the government had to deal with each other, their interactions were characterized more by discord than by reconciliation. USAID had compromised its ability to act as an honest broker because of its reliance on the SRN. As an evaluation conducted by Development Associates, Inc., observed, "Had USAID not put all of its eggs in the SRN basket, it might have been in a position to serve as a facilitator in bringing the two sides together; tripartite (or quadripartite with ONUSAL) planning could have been fostered in place of the bilateral, frequently acrimonious, negotiations that actually have taken place."[48]

The decision to channel assistance through the SRN may also have weakened the design of programs. USAID/El Salvador initially planned to limit targeted assistance to demobilized troops and to integrate them into programs for the general population in the former conflictive zones. It also intended to provide benefits directly to former combatants, rather than go through the FAES or the FMLN. These two approaches were unsatisfactory in the view of both groups, which sought to control the distribution of benefits to their own troops to gain political advantage.

However, the FMLN's position may also have reflected an unwillingness to collaborate with the agency responsible for the government's economic counterinsurgency efforts.

USAID/El Salvador's experience raises the question of the continuity of mission personnel during the transition phase. There clearly is a trade-off between, on the one hand, keeping personnel so as to retain their knowledge of the local situation, their contacts, and the confidence of the sitting government and, on the other hand, bringing in staff who have a fresh approach and are not tainted by wartime connections and associations. It is not, of course, necessary to change staff in order to change policy, because a good deal can be achieved by issuing clear instructions from headquarters and monitoring staff closely. USAID/El Salvador, for example, initially was wary of collaborating with NGOs that had been affiliated with the FMLN during the war. Following a change in administrations in the United States, which produced new instructions from Washington that were relayed clearly, forcefully, and frequently, the USAID mission became a good deal more supportive of those NGOs.

IMPACT OF POLITICS ON PROGRAM DESIGN AND IMPLEMENTATION

Political considerations can determine the content of peacebuilding programs in ways that foreclose options that, under other circumstances, might seem to be advantageous. This is, in essence, what occurred when the FMLN and the FAES vetoed USAID's plan to include demobilized soldiers in programs aimed at reactivating the economy of the zones of conflict and demanded instead programs targeted specifically to former combatants. Development Associates, Inc., has noted that, "the proposed USAID strategy which was rejected by the two sides would likely have resulted in more, and certainly more relevant, benefits being provided to the ex-combatants more rapidly and in a manner that would have been more promotive of reconciliation."[49]

Maximizing the welfare of former combatants was not a high priority for either the FMLN or the FAES. Rather, both sought to control their former soldiers for as long as possible. The FAES wanted to control the benefits process to prevent an external body from verifying the size of its troops once demobilization was completed. Control was also a relic of the counterinsurgency mentality. To counterbalance FMLN-controlled communities in the former conflictive zones, the FAES on several occasions established communities populated by its own former soldiers in the same localities. In this circumstance, allowing soldiers to determine where they wanted to settle or what training they wanted to pursue would have been counterproductive.[50] For its part, the FMLN saw an electoral advantage in controlling the distribution of benefits to its former troops. (The government, of course, was able to gain its own electoral advantage by controlling the distribution of funds through the SRN.)

Although it may be difficult to overcome these political impediments to program design, donors need to be aware that such impediments exist and maximize their ability to be viewed as honest brokers.

The political environment in which peacebuilding efforts occur can also be an impediment to program implementation. The provisions of peace accords are frequently interdependent; actions taken in one area often depend on compliance in another. As a result, programs to implement the provisions of peace accords are often tightly linked. The difficulty of achieving a level of mutual trust that enables parties to take steps that are extremely sensitive politically often throws program implementation off course.[51]

In El Salvador, for example, the main vehicle for reintegrating demobilized FMLN combatants was to be the land transfer program. When both the demobilization process and implementation of the land transfer program fell behind schedule, approximately 80 percent of FMLN soldiers missed the 1992 planting season. It then became necessary to develop a basic agricultural training program rapidly to replace the technical assistance program for ongoing agricultural activities that had originally been planned.[52] Situations such as this underscore the importance of keeping programs flexible and planning for contingencies.

IMPACT OF POLITICS ON DONORS' OPERATING PROCEDURES

Donors have often been insensitive to the political complexities of peacebuilding activities, viewing them initially as technical problems that should be solved in the most efficient manner. For example, when charged with establishing a technical mission to oversee the creation of the El Salvador police training academy, the National Academy of Public Security, UNDP brought together technical experts from the two major donor countries, Spain and the United States, to work with the Government of El Salvador. It initially neglected to consult the FMLN.[53] Although this oversight was rapidly corrected once the FMLN complained, it created additional ill will that could easily have been avoided.

The traditional ways in which donors conduct business often do not satisfy the needs of peacebuilding. For example, UNDP normally acts as an adviser to governments. It rarely works with nongovernmental entities or implements projects directly. However, its participation in peacebuilding activities has required UNDP to work with opposition groups and NGOs in addition to governments. On some occasions, UNDP has had to assume a direct role in implementing projects (see Box 16).

BOX 16. IMPLEMENTING THE REINTEGRATION SUPPORT SCHEME IN MOZAMBIQUE

The Reintegration Support Scheme was part of the ex-combatant reintegration program in Mozambique. It provided 18 months of severance pay to some 91,000 soldiers demobilized under the auspices of the U.N. operation in Mozambique. Payments were available in bimonthly installments to veterans who presented vouchers and a demobilization card at the branch of the Banco Popular de Desenvolvimento (BPD) closest to the his or her home district.

The responsibility for implementation and financial management of the program resided with UNDP, which was responsible for accounting, reporting, and auditing financial operations. As part of this process, the UNDP provided the BPD with lists of demobilized soldiers eligible to obtain payments through each branch, the amount each veteran was to be paid, and the dates during which he or she could receive each of the nine payments.

The resident mission in Maputo understood the importance of such tasks and was willing to undertake them. But according to U.N. officials, UNDP headquarters in New York did not want to assume responsibility for the program. The objections were twofold: first, UNDP's mandate is to promote development, and providing severance pay to former combatants does not constitute a development program; and second, UNDP is not an implementing agency and should therefore not become directly involved in project execution.

Source: Authors' interviews.

The departure from traditional roles has created tensions between headquarters and field missions and between field missions and their traditional client governments.

The donor community is making an effort to extract the lessons from recent peacebuilding experiences and to apply them to new situations. Studies of the lessons learned and best practices are one of the main mechanisms employed for transmitting experiences. The World Bank's 1993 study on demobilization and reintegration filled an enormous gap and has been in considerable demand from practitioners. It also stimulated considerable follow-on research and meetings to exchange information, including in-depth field reviews conducted by the World Bank of the experiences of three African countries. The conclusions of this second round of World Bank studies have also been much in demand, even prior to their formal publication.[54]

Similarly, resident bilateral and multilateral aid missions have reviewed various aspects of specific peacebuilding experiences. UNDP/El Salvador commissioned a report from a group of independent analysts on the challenges of combining war-to-peace transitions with far-reaching economic reform. USAID/El Salvador assessed its own contribution to peacebuilding in that country with a view to extracting lessons for future USAID-supported peacebuilding activities. Study visits can also be helpful, such as the one in which staff of the USAID mission in El Salvador and Salvadoran government officials examined demobilization experiences in Colombia and Nicaragua.

Another method of learning from the past is to involve personnel with previous experience in war-torn countries in the planning and implementation of subsequent peace processes. In 1994-95, the United Nations shifted some ONUSAL personnel from El Salvador to Guatemala in anticipation of a peace process there.[55] Similarly, the United Nations transferred to Angola some of the individuals involved in Mozambique's peace process. Individuals transferred in this way should give due weight to the differences in national circumstances.

Donors need to do more, however, than simply take the lessons of one peace process and apply them to the next. They need to inculcate in their staff the importance of incorporating the political dimension into their analyses and of bearing in mind political obstacles to the programs they develop.[56] Although operating in a political vacuum is never desirable, doing so is particularly problematic in post-conflict environments.

. . . .

MODE OF DELIVERING ASSISTANCE

"There was one deficiency in the whole peace process: The donors were so coordinated; we were all focused on compliance with the General Peace Agreement, its timetable, the elections. Too little attention was given to contacts with the Mozambique government. . . . The donors are extremely mistrustful of the government and the temptation to bypass the government is very strong. [But] they need to fight that tendency and try to be flexible."

—Senior diplomat, Maputo, Mozambique, January 1995

■   WHEN WARS END, governments are typically seriously overextended and unable to fulfill key functions and deliver critical services. The opposition, which retains control of its weapons through a portion of the transition phase, remains wary of the government. Opposition leaders frequently believe that the government will fail to deliver benefits in an equitable fashion and seek to limit the government's role in peacebuilding activities in areas formerly under their control. At the same time, there is significant pressure to implement peacebuilding programs rapidly.

These conditions present donors with a dilemma. In order to implement peacebuilding activities, resources can be channeled either through the government or through nongovernmental bodies and international organizations. Where wars end without a victor, the sitting government is simultaneously the government and one of the factions seeking political power in the period prior to the election. Under any circumstance, governments of war-torn countries aspire to fulfill the functions of government but lack adequate capacity. In addition, they may have ceded certain responsibilities to a peacekeeping operation. Consequently, donors often believe that bypassing the government is desirable in the name of efficiency and impartiality.

This short-term strategy may, however, create significant problems in the medium to long term. If donors postpone significant institution strengthening and capacity building until a new government is elected and rely on nongovernmental bodies to design and execute peacebuilding programs, the post-election government probably will be no more prepared to carry out key tasks than was the preelection government. Indeed, since the transition phase generally lasts between 18 months and two years, governments may well enter the consolidation phase with their capacity for independent action severely weakened. Cambodia offers an excellent example of the hazards of this approach (see Box 17). Yet, as El Salvador demonstrates, the result of making the government the main vehicle of peacebuilding assistance can be equally problematic. Assistance may be used to gain electoral advantage at the expense of the most war-affected groups, fostering a political environment inimical to reconciliation.

BOX 17. DONOR NEUTRALITY IN CAMBODIA

"As urged by the U.S. and France, both UNTAC and the bilateral donor agencies adhered to a restrictive definition of political 'neutrality' prior to the elections, when it came to dealing with the existing bureaucracy, apart from activities to facilitate the election. Accepting the argument that this bureaucracy was beholden to the SOC faction [State of Cambodia, that is, the ruling Cambodian People's Party], and potentially a SOC instrument for influencing the vote, the donors beginning to be active inside Cambodia severely constrained UNTAC's rehabilitation component and refused to provide aid through the bureaucracy. They refused financial support that would have enabled the SOC to restore its collapsed capacity to pay civil servant salaries. . . . NGOs and international agencies (like UNICEF) that had been working to begin a restoration of Cambodia's devastated education, health, and other social services in the 1980s were not in position to prevent the renewed deterioration resulting from this politically driven policy of the transition arrangements.

"One cannot know what effects on the election outcome might have resulted if the 'neutrality' policy had allowed for budget support during the UNTAC period, especially in the months immediately prior to the elections. It is clear, however, that the more than two years between a) the collapse of Soviet aid and the budget support that had entailed and b) the start of IFI [international financial institution] aid for the RCG [Royal Cambodian Government] budget had significant negative consequences for the post–May 1993 reconstruction and reconciliation processes that were designed to dovetail with legitimation."

Source: Frederick Z. Brown and Robert J. Muscat, "The Transition from War to Peace: The Case of Cambodia," paper prepared for the Overseas Development Council Program on Enhancing Security and Development (Washington, DC, March 14, 1995), pp. 66–67.

What is necessary, although extremely difficult to achieve, is a nuanced approach that progressively strengthens central government's capacity to carry out key activities but minimizes its capacity to use resources for partisan political purposes.

A first step in this process might be to establish a forum in which donors and governments discuss the following issues: 1) the overall policy framework within which peacebuilding activities will occur; 2) the key tasks for government, a priority ranking of tasks, and the appropriate level of government to assume responsibility for each task; 3) methods of incorporating input both from the former armed opposition and, more broadly, from civil society; and 4) the specific roles that different donor agencies will play in helping to implement peacebuilding programs, both prior to and following elections. Where appropriate, government agencies or public sector entities could implement programs under the close financial monitoring of donor agencies.

Where donors are already supporting efforts to build capacity and strengthen institutions, it might be possible to incorporate peacebuilding objectives into these efforts soon after the accords are signed. Similarly, ongoing decentralization activities could be linked to peacebuilding at the local level. One possibility worth investigating is the extent to which local committees composed of government representatives, community leaders, representatives of local NGOs, businessmen, and local citizens could be constituted to provide input on a range of issues pertaining to the design and implementation of peacebuilding projects and programs. In some post-conflict countries where this system has been employed, such as Cambodia, community groups have shown themselves capable of assuming full responsibility for managing community rehabilitation projects such as repairing roads, bridges, and irrigation systems. This included financial management.

There are, of course, problems associated with such local committees. The first is that the committees frequently require assistance in prioritizing needs. A second problem is organizational: Someone has to set the process in motion. Identifying committee members, ensuring that committees are reasonably representative, and helping members to prioritize community needs are undeniably time-consuming. In some countries, such as Mozambique, where the legacy of centralized rule includes forced collaboration, the positive aspects of community action may be poorly understood, particularly in rural areas where memories of efforts to force farmers into communal villages are still vivid. Despite such problems, it is worthwhile determining, in consultation with individuals familiar with each locality, whether pilot projects are feasible. In this respect, it is important to recall that what is not feasible in one part of a country or one sector of the economy may suit conditions elsewhere.

ENGAGING THE NONGOVERNMENTAL SECTOR

Irrespective of the amount of capacity building and institution strengthening that takes place, the nongovernmental sector will inevitably be engaged during the transition phase. Several observations are in order about the role of NGOs in peacebuilding efforts.

MANAGING NGOS. Both international and local NGOs that have been active in the country for some time can contribute importantly to the development and execution of peacebuilding programs through their knowledge of and relationship with local populations. At the same time, peacebuilding has become a growth industry and is attracting more and more international nongovernmental agencies with limited local knowledge and insufficient expertise in the areas central to peacebuilding. The proliferation of NGOs and the tendency of many to act autonomously cause problems for both the donors and the host government. The government is particularly ill-equipped to track, let alone manage, the activities of the hundreds of NGOs that are typically active in post-conflict countries.

This situation has led to proposals for a code of conduct for NGOs. Issues covered by such a code might include mechanisms for coordinating NGO activities, agreement on standardized salaries for local staff, commitment to local capacity building, and the development of timely and appropriate exit strategies. Funding from donors would depend on adherence to the code of conduct. Desirable as such a method of regulating NGO behavior would be, negotiating a code of conduct could be quite time-consuming. In the interim, it is clear that donors need to enhance their oversight of NGO activities. A review of rehabilitation efforts in the health sector concluded that donors "are often reactive to NGO proposals, not proactive in setting guidelines for NGO engagement."[57] One means of becoming more proactive would be to require donors to have each NGO that receives their funding sign a memorandum of understanding governing its actions. At the very least, donors should be extremely selective about the private agencies they fund.

An additional consideration is that some of the key objectives of peacebuilding—enhancing reconciliation and participation and improving the condition of economically marginalized groups—can complicate the capacity of donors to manage their implementing agencies. With regard to El Salvador, the World Bank has noted that, "while donor support mobilized through the CG [Consultative Group] process is essential to the success of the government's reconstruction objectives, the community-based approach of many of the NRP (National Reconstruction Plan) initiatives makes overall coordination more problematic. Moreover, some donors have preferred to channel their assistance directly through NGOs or beneficiary groups, which makes it more difficult to keep track of coverage and impact."[58]

At a minimum, each donor should encourage coordination among the implementing agencies it funds in each sector. In El Salvador, for example, NGOs funded by USAID to develop village banking projects were not coordinated, which led to an unequal geographical coverage. Where relevant and feasible, donors should also support local initiatives, such as the municipal coordination of NGOs in Nejapa and the Local Economic Development Agency programs in Chalatenango and Morazán provinces in El Salvador.

DEVELOPING LOCAL CAPACITY. Many local NGOs do not have the managerial or substantive capacity to play a major role in designing or implementing programs. By assisting them to upgrade their skills in these crucial areas, donors can help these organizations to modulate their political positions and become less partisan.

One mechanism that has been employed with some success is the so-called umbrella program. Grants or loans are provided to an NGO (often, but not necessarily, an international NGO) with a proven track record. This NGO takes responsibility for distributing resources to grassroots organizations as well as for handling the administrative, managerial, and financial aspects of the project. The grassroots organizations receive technical assistance designed to enhance their capacity to receive grants independently. The umbrella mechanism greatly reduces the administrative burdens of the funding agency. In El Salvador, umbrella programs have been employed to strengthen opposition NGOs that operated in the conflict zones during the war and need assistance to improve their technical capacity, including financial management.[59]

Another mechanism for supporting NGOs that lack financial management capabilities is for the entity distributing the funds to contract with or provide a grant to an institution that will train the NGO staff in financial management. Donors can also provide funds through fixed-price contracts that require achievement of an objective in a specified period of time. Some money is provided up-front and the remainder of the funds are disbursed according to agreed benchmarks. This greatly simplifies monitoring, because financial management capability is not at issue. Rather, the institution's ability to carry out the project in the time allotted is what counts.[60]

Training and institutional-strengthening programs are also an option, although the length of time needed to develop the capacity to design and execute a project suggests that this may not be the most appropriate use of resources. Such programs may be more helpful for NGOs that already have a certain capacity and need to sharpen specific aspects of their performance, for example through short seminars designed to enhance particular skills. For NGOs that need to transform their organizational character, a more hands-on approach may be desirable.

REINVENTING NGOS. Even local NGOs that were closely linked to local populations during wartime are not always the mechanism through which local communities choose to promote rehabilitation and reconciliation. NGOs created for one purpose—supporting local populations under difficult wartime conditions—almost invariably need to transform themselves to meet the peacetime needs of local communities. In El Salvador, for example, opposition NGOs need to improve their ability to deliver technical support and become more open to participatory planning and decision making (see Box 18).[61]

A DELICATE BALANCE: STRENGTHENING CIVIL SOCIETY AND GOVERNMENT

Strengthening NGOs can help to build civil society, enhance opportunities for participation, and foster political reconciliation. Similarly, involving private enterprises in rehabilitation, reconstruction, and development can strengthen their capacity to generate employment and provide goods and services at affordable rates. Therefore, identifying those areas in which private sector actors have an appropriate role to play is highly desirable. However, bypassing the government simply because it is inefficient or because it represents a wartime faction may erode the

---

BOX 18. REINVENTING "OPPOSITION" NGOS IN EL SALVADOR

"During the war, the opposition NGOs were charged with carrying out dangerous projects. . . . Working in the war zones in support of a civilian population identified by the government as the FMLN's 'social base' implied a certain set of relations with the main actors in the conflict—the FMLN and the Salvadoran armed forces—that very much affected institutional priorities.

"With peace, all of these circumstances have changed radically. . . . In one way or another, all of the opposition NGOs have begun a 'conversion' process designed to adjust to these changes. Not only do their constituents have different needs, but their key sources of support—international NGOs—

also see this new period in a different light.

"The major changes being demanded of these NGOs in this transition period include 1) improved, more transparent financial administration; 2) increased capacity to provide technical support to communities; 3) decentralization away from the capital and toward the communities and more participatory planning and decision making; 4) longer-term planning oriented toward regional solutions.

". . . Predictably, not all community leaders are happy with the pace at which these changes are happening in the NGOs, and tensions between communities and NGOs have increased accordingly."

—Kevin Murray et al., *Rescuing Reconstruction: The Debate on Post-War Economic Recovery in El Salvador* (Cambridge, MA, and San Salvador: Hemisphere Initiatives, May 1994), p. 19.

government's capacity and undermine its ability to fulfill the functions that governments must fulfill. In addition, decentralization should not be pursued at the expense of a central government that is capable of establishing broad policy frameworks and delineating government priorities in key sectors. The challenge, therefore, is to find the appropriate blend of actors and determine what role each of them is best suited to play in the peacebuilding process.

The precise role of government will vary from country to country, depending in large part on the country's level of development and the efficiency of the public administrative sector. The traditional roles of government have been defined as "maintaining law and order; providing a just legal framework under which households and private firms will produce and trade goods and services; investing in and maintaining physical and social infrastructure; and promoting agricultural research and extension."[62] Most post-conflict countries are incapable of fulfilling these roles. A central objective of the donors during both the transition and the consolidation phases should be to strengthen government's capacity to undertake these activities.

. . . .

COORDINATION

"No one wanted to be coordinated."
—U.N. official, El Salvador, September 1994

■ WARS CREATE THE CONDITIONS in which fundamental political and economic restructuring can occur. The necessity of acting rapidly to take advantage of these relatively short-lived opportunities places a premium on the coordination of aid for both the international community and host government. Aid is notoriously difficult to coordinate, even in countries that are not emerging from lengthy civil wars.[63] In post-conflict countries, both the needs and the problems are magnified. In particular, the aftereffects of protracted civil wars enhance the political considerations that can hinder coordination.

Coordination is required at various levels: within the individual institutions and agencies that constitute the international community, among the ministries and agencies of bilateral donor governments, among the ministries and agencies of the host government, within the international community, and between the international community and the host government.

Enhanced coordination within donor countries (also known as policy coherence) has long been an objective of the OECD Development Assistance Committee in its efforts to make aid resources more effective. It has become increasingly important as countries have become more interdependent and their relations more complex and as the range of global concerns has expanded to include issues such as human rights, environmental protection, migration, and post-conflict reconstruction. The expansion of donor involvement in post-war environments has underscored the serious conflicts of interest that exist within development cooperation agencies and between these agencies and other members of the international community. Many officials in both bilateral and multilateral donor institutions view peacebuilding activities as a diversion of resources from "true" development objectives rather than as the crucial foundation for sustainable development that they actually are. Military establishments are often loath to see their resources applied to rehabilitation and reconstruction. These and other turf battles are magnified by shrinking budgets.

This section focuses on two aspects of post-conflict coordination: coordination among donors during the transition phase of the peace process and coordination by governments of war-torn countries.

DONOR COORDINATION IN THE TRANSITION PHASE

It is vital for donors to coordinate their activities throughout the entire peace process, but coordination is especially critical during the transition phase. This period is typically characterized by tight timetables and the need to incorporate new actors such as the former armed opposition and a U.N. peacekeeping force as well as a large number of external agencies. The ability of donors to adapt to these new conditions will greatly enhance the effectiveness of their aid.

MULTIFUNCTIONAL PEACEKEEPING OPERATIONS. One factor that complicates donor coordination in the immediate post-conflict period is the arrival of a multifunctional peacekeeping operation, which, ironically, is intended to facilitate coordination (see Box 19). Both formal and informal mechanisms for donor coordination are likely to be in existence when peacekeeping operations are established, and the failure to take these preexisting mechanisms into account for whatever reason creates considerable ill will. These feelings will be intensified if the special representative of the U.N. secretary-general (SRSG) is overburdened by the political and military aspects of the peace process, leaving him or her with little time to oversee the humanitarian aspects of peacebuilding.

The U.N. operation in Mozambique was one of the first peacekeeping missions that attempted to maintain direct control over the coordination of humanitarian assistance by requesting that the U.N. Department of Humanitarian Affairs establish a special unit—the U.N. Office of Humanitarian Assistance Coordination (UNOHAC)—within the peacekeeping mission. In doing so, it earned the resentment of UNDP, which felt that UNOHAC had usurped the mandate of its resident representative who was also the U.N. resident coordinator, and the resentment of much of the bilateral donor community, which viewed UNOHAC as an unnecessary layer of bureaucracy. The independent working style of the first UNOHAC director only added to this resentment. Consequently, relations between much of the local donor community and UNOHAC deteriorated sharply during 1993. The SRSG's capacity to influence this situation was limited, in large part because he was consumed with the task of creating an environment in which elections could go forward.

BOX 19. THE SPECIAL REPRESENTATIVE OF THE SECRETARY-GENERAL AS COORDINATOR

"When operational activities for development are undertaken within the context of a peacekeeping mission, which is placed under the command of a special representative, all elements of the United Nations system at all levels that are active in the theatre of operations must come under the command and direction of the special representative. It must be recognized that the special representative has not only a political but also an essential coordinating role in this regard."

—U.N. General Assembly, *An Agenda for Development: Recommendations. Report of the Secretary-General*, document A/49/665 (New York: United Nations, November 11, 1994), p. 15, para. 89.

The international community urgently needs to consider how much responsibility should be placed on the shoulders of one individual and whether a person who is well suited to see that the parties comply with the peace accords in a politically charged atmosphere has either the time or the expertise to oversee peacebuilding efforts.

When the SRSG in Mozambique gave his full attention to a problem, obstacles were generally overcome. When he did not, the outcome was considerably less certain. At the very beginning of the U.N. Observer Mission in Mozambique (ONUMOZ), the special representative obtained the support he needed from the Mozambican parties to proceed with a demining program. He was forced, however, to turn his attention to more pressing matters, and UNOHAC assumed responsibility for the demining program. Progress slowed to a crawl, leading many donors to criticize severely UNOHAC's handling of the program. In contrast, the special representative was strongly committed to creating a political environment conducive to holding elections and consulted closely with donor governments on this issue. The donors felt that coordination on electoral assistance functioned very well.

ALTERNATIVE MECHANISMS FOR COORDINATION. The foregoing discussion suggests that although it is, in principle, desirable for the SRSG to oversee the entire range of activities necessary to implement the provisions of the peace accords in the transition phase, adding a layer of U.N. bureaucracy to coordinate external assistance for peacebuilding activities may not be the most efficient means of coordinating among the donors. Rather, it would be desirable to build to the extent possible on what already exists on the ground, including U.N. and other multilateral agencies, bilateral donors, or ad hoc entities.

One alternative to integrating a coordinating mechanism into the peacekeeping operation itself would be to vest the powers of donor coordination with the U.N. resident coordinator, generally the UNDP resident representative. This was the situation in El Salvador, where the resident UNDP mission retained responsibility for coordinating humanitarian assistance and was given new responsibilities, under chapter V of the peace accords, for programs to implement provisions of the accords. Specifically, UNDP was charged with advising the Government on all matters relating to the mobilization of external support, assisting in the preparation of projects and programmes likely to attract such support, facilitating approaches to official bilateral and multilateral agencies, mobilizing technical assistance and cooperating with the Government in harmonizing the Plan with the activities of nongovernmental organizations involved in local and regional development activities.[64]

This model experienced several problems, notably uncertainty about the precise lines of authority between the U.N. peacekeeping mission, ONUSAL, and UNDP that contributed, particularly at the beginning of the peace process, to misunderstandings and delays in program execution and the desire of each donor to retain maximum autonomy over its programs (see Box 20). Crises, such as the emergency program for provisioning FMLN combatants in troop assembly areas, produced close collaboration, but this evaporated once the crisis was over. UNDP lacked the financial clout that might have compelled greater cooperation, at least within the U.N. system.

The El Salvador experience strongly suggests that a more formal link between the SRSG and the resident donor community is needed. One mechanism worth exploring would be to appoint the U.N. resident

BOX 20. U.N. COORDINATION IN EL SALVADOR

"The U.N. is an institution with several related parts, but outsiders frequently underestimate the institutional barriers and rivalries that mitigate against closer collaboration. Compared to other major peacekeeping efforts, the relationships among U.N. organizations in El Salvador on the whole were comparatively positive. However, at the outset of the peace process, there were two quite separate systems: ONUSAL and its components and the regular U.N. agencies that had been there before and would remain after the peace mission departed. The peace process in El Salvador benefited from the fact that these two systems—and the donors—shared similar assumptions and managed to work cooperatively. Nevertheless, much of what was accomplished was unplanned and came about thanks mainly to good will, flexibility on the ground, and the willingness of donors to back peace initiatives."

—Patricia Weiss Fagen, "El Salvador: Lessons in Peace Consolidation," in *Beyond Sovereignty: Collectively Defending Democracy in the Americas*, ed. Tom Farer (Baltimore, MD: Johns Hopkins University Press, 1996).

coordinator as the SRSG's deputy for peacebuilding activities, supported by a coordinating committee composed of members of the resident donor missions. In the absence of a UNDP Resident Representative, this function could be fulfilled by the World Bank Resident Representative or a senior bilateral donor official. This would have the virtue of creating a formal mechanism through which the institutions expected to finance the peace accords could participate in shaping programs from the beginning and would enhance cooperation during the very critical transition phase. It also could provide a direct channel for incorporating the views of the government, the armed opposition, and representatives of civil society into the process if, for example, the forum for donors and the government described earlier were created and linked to the donor coordinating committee.

The committee could designate one of its members as lead donor in each area in which the parties to the conflict require assistance in implementing the peace accords: electoral process, demobilization and reintegration of former combatants, police reform, demining, rehabilitation, and so on. Each lead donor would work with the parties to develop specific proposals for the donor community. Part of the mandate of the lead donor would be to solicit the views and proposals of civil society. In countries where donor coordination is normally carried out under the auspices of a Consultative Group, the World Bank should perhaps take the lead in economic and social recovery programs. For Round Table countries, the UNDP could assume that role.

For this model to work, there clearly has to be agreement at the highest levels among UNDP, a Department of Political Affairs, and the U.N. Office of the Secretary-General about the division of labor and authority between the SRSG and the resident coordinator and between UNDP and the other members of the U.N. family. (Where, as in Bosnia, responsibility for the peacekeeping mission resides outside the United Nations, a similar agreement would be necessary among the appropriate institutions.) This agreement needs to be communicated clearly to the relevant actors and reinforced as necessary. In addition, the resident donor community would have to reach agreement on relations among donors before the peace accords are signed. Because peace agreements typically take several years to negotiate, there is ample time for the details of these relationships to be worked out before a peacekeeping mission arrives.

This mechanism would provide for the smoothest move from the transition to the consolidation phase. One of the problems that have arisen when a U.N. peacekeeping operation has complete or significant authority over peacebuilding activities during the transition phase is the difficulty of transferring its responsibilities to local donors when the peacekeeping mission reaches the end of its mandate. In this case, the organizations responsible for peacebuilding activities during both the transition and the consolidation phases would be one and the same. Nonetheless, hand-off strategies would have to be developed from the inception of the peacekeeping operation.

COORDINATION BY GOVERNMENTS OF POST-CONFLICT COUNTRIES

The efficient use of aid resources requires not only that donors coordinate their activities but also that host governments coordinate the inflow of external financing.[65] This is desirable not only to avoid unnecessary duplication of efforts (although such duplication may fulfill a commercial or political purpose for donors and recipients) but also to enable governments to mesh the activities of donors with national priorities.

As a first step, governments require detailed information about the nature and extent of the external financing they receive. A seemingly straightforward requirement, the governments of post-conflict countries frequently need to build the capacity to collect and manage these data. In addition, donors may need to be convinced of the need to be more transparent about the resources they provide (see Box 21). In Nicaragua, after years of discussion about the desirability of creating a computerized database of donor-financed projects and programs, no concrete results have been recorded.

Beyond simply tracking the inflow of aid, recipient governments have sometimes sought to centralize the management of external resources. Recent evaluations of countries that have used their aid resources effectively strongly suggest that "a well-staffed and centrally located aid coordination unit, in regular contact with sector departments

"The Mozambican authorities have been trying for some time to set up and maintain a data base on foreign aid inflows and uses. Enhancements of this data base are needed to permit the government to report with more transparency and accuracy on the breakdown between investment and current expenditure and on public expenditures by sector. To carry out these improvements, the government will need the collaboration of the donor community in regularly providing detailed information on foreign aid flows and uses. Please make your best efforts to collaborate. It is important."

—Mozambique Consultative Group Meeting, "Statement of the Staff Representative of the International Monetary Fund" (Paris, March 14–15, 1965).

and aid agencies" is a crucial component of aid management.[66] Because of resource constraints, post-conflict countries face special challenges in making aid coordination units function properly. In particular, the possibility that the coordination unit will usurp the functions of the line ministries seems to be especially large. Following the 1994 genocidal civil war in Rwanda, the new government created the ministry of rehabilitation to oversee the resettlement of refugees and internally displaced persons and the rehabilitation of the economy. This ministry has sidelined many of the technically competent line ministries, going so far as to write a resettlement plan without consulting those that remain. In the estimation of some donors, this has reduced the efficiency with which resources are being used.

This outcome does not invalidate the concept of a centralized aid coordination unit in post-conflict countries, but it does suggest that donors need to take steps to prevent the emergence of imbalances between that unit and the line ministries. In particular, donors need to be careful not to focus their resources disproportionately on the coordination unit. They also need to monitor the activities of the coordination unit and communicate with relevant government officials if the coordination unit is beginning to act autonomously. If dialogue does not achieve the desired results and donors think that aid resources are being used inefficiently, they should consider the possibility of limiting their support of the coordination unit.

Part V
Agenda for the Future

NEXT STEPS

■ AS THE FOREGOING DISCUSSION SUGGESTS, there are a considerable number of areas in which the donors and other members of the international community could usefully take action to improve the effectiveness of their assistance to post-conflict peacebuilding efforts. The following section proposes a number of priorities for donors in two areas: 1) issues that can be addressed immediately, and 2) areas where gaps in current understanding argue strongly in favor of further analysis.

. . . .
IMMEDIATE ACTIONS

Donors should foster the understanding within their organizations that peacebuilding activities are a critical precondition for development in post-conflict environments. Just as donors often view war itself as an externality—a relatively self-contained event of fairly short duration—development practitioners frequently view assistance that helps war-torn countries to overcome the effects of armed conflict as a diversion of resources from the real business of development. Indeed, it is sometimes argued that promoting development is the most effective means of promoting peace.

In reality, if the economic, political, social, and security imbalances that both produced the war and resulted from it are not addressed during the transition phase of the peace process, resources devoted to development may be wasted. It is therefore vital that senior management transmit two messages to their staff. A return to traditional development activities in the near term in post-conflict environments is neither possible nor desirable. Equally important, priority must be given to addressing the three broad objectives of peacebuilding: building political institutions, enhancing internal and external security, and promoting economic and social revitalization.

Donors should take steps to extend the time horizon of peacebuilding activities. At present, few donors look more than two or three years into the future. However, to be effective, peacebuilding efforts must adopt a considerably longer time frame. In pledging to support peacebuilding efforts in a specific country, donors are not committing themselves to provide high levels of financial outlays throughout the entire period. While financial requirements will certainly increase, particularly during the transition phase, it is unrealistic in this era of chronic donor fatigue to assume that donors will be able to sustain a high level of financial support. Equally important, the relative balance between financial support, technical assistance, and policy dialogue will shift over time and according to objective. Donors are, however, committing themselves to a sustained effort to foster the adoption of policies and patterns of behavior that will minimize disparities among social groups and maximize the opportunities for resolving disputes peacefully.

Senior management therefore needs to indicate clearly that the planning cycle for war-torn countries will be longer in the future. Senior management also needs to examine current planning practices and guidelines to eliminate possible impediments to adopting this longer time frame. The difficulty in committing funds for any length of time, project cycles that last a maximum of three years, and the need for immediate results are some of the constraints that should be addressed.

To maximize the effectiveness of the external resources invested in peacebuilding, a division of labor urgently needs to be established both between donors and other members of the international community and among donors themselves. Many of the tasks for external actors that are generated by peacebuilding activities are appropriately undertaken by institutions outside the development community, such as foreign, defense, and justice ministries and regional organizations. Some tasks that are within the mandate of the international development community—such as demobilization and reintegration of former soldiers or truth commissions—require diplomatic support to be fully effective. Each donor has a comparative advantage in certain activities. Despite considerable rhetoric about the importance of coordination, in all too many cases, battles over institutional turf prevail over the development of collaborative relationships. This both undermines the effectiveness of resources invested in peacebuilding and damages the long-term prospects of war-torn societies. In consequence, there needs to be an effort to ensure that the commitment, at senior levels, to supporting peacebuilding tasks is transmitted clearly and consistently to staff both at headquarters and in the field. In addition, mechanisms should be developed to reinforce the preference for institutional collaboration.

To improve the efficiency and quality of their support for peacebuilding efforts, donors should 1) develop cooperative relations with the parties to the conflict as early in the peace process as possible to enable meaningful planning to begin before the peace accords are signed; 2) enhance the flexibility of their funding; 3) ensure that personnel are carefully matched to the jobs to which they are assigned; 4) incorporate into program design the evaluation of political obstacles to achieving objectives; and 5) hold implementing agencies accountable. Although most of these requirements pertain to assistance provided under other circumstances, the need is greater in post-conflict environments. An examination of recent peacebuilding efforts indicates that more often than not these characteristics have been conspicuous by their absence and that this has served to blunt the effectiveness of donor assistance in post-conflict situations. Although most of these changes will take time to implement completely, senior management should begin to lay the groundwork for them immediately. If, for example, approval of the legislature or managing board is required to obtain waivers that make post-conflict funding more flexible, steps should be taken to bring the issue before these bodies at the earliest possible moment. Similarly, discussions should begin within donors on the behavior expected of implementing agencies, and a procedure should be outlined for incorporating these guidelines into agreements with the implementing agencies.

Donors should use informal policy dialogue and formal performance criteria to press the parties to comply fully with the obligations they have assumed under the terms of the peace agreement. Following the signing of the peace accords, each of the parties to the conflict makes every effort to reinterpret the agreement to its own advantage and to use its compliance (or noncompliance) as leverage over the other signatories. In particular, governments of war-torn countries frequently take refuge behind the concept of sovereignty to justify their failure to comply with the peace accords. However, the traditional concept of sovereignty loses a good deal of its weight in post-conflict situations where no one party has emerged victorious and where the government has ceded certain of its responsibilities to an international peacekeeping mission. The international community has both the right and the obligation to press the parties to comply fully with the provisions of the peace accords. At the same time, the international community and its constituent members have a responsibility to exert this pressure in a manner consistent with the spirit of the peace accords rather than to seek partisan gains.

Donors should make every effort to ensure that peacebuilding activities enhance reconciliation. Two key objectives in this regard are 1) to create conditions in which the parties to the conflict focus on solving specific problems rather than on continuing their efforts to dominate one another, and 2) to increase the opportunities for participation by civil society. The creation of issue-oriented working groups at all stages of the peace process could be a useful mechanism for attaining both these goals. Incorporating the voices of civil society is admittedly difficult, because a major characteristic of war-torn countries is the paucity of effective civil society organizations and the politicization of those that do exist. Nonetheless, donors need to make a special effort to see that the voices of civil society are included to the greatest extent possible in discussions both about the terms of the peace accords and their implementation.

In view of the institutional weaknesses of post-conflict societies, donors need to give priority to building capacity in both the public sector and within civil society as early in the peacebuilding stage as possible. In the public sector, the objectives would be to identify key tasks of government, to prioritize those tasks according to time and the appropriate government implementing agency, and to determine what assistance government will need to increase its capacity to carry out these tasks independently and in an apolitical manner. For civil society, the objectives would be to enhance the capacity of relevant organizations to evaluate policy and to develop and implement programs in their respective spheres of activity.

ISSUES FOR FURTHER CONSIDERATION

The current transition phase, which normally lasts between one and two years, is too short, and holding elections so soon after the termination of hostilities tends to close the reform process prematurely. It would accordingly be useful to examine how long and under what conditions the transition phase could be extended. One of the lessons that the international community has learned from recent peace processes is that winner-take-all elections can delay the achievement of stability, reconciliation, and political development. In consequence, the international community has sought to convince post-conflict countries to adopt governments of national unity. Installing such governments as a result of elections does not, however, resolve the problem of premature closure, and such governments are difficult to graft onto peace agreements after the fact. Additional options should therefore be considered, such as installation of an interim, caretaker government, established for a specific period of time with a mandate to begin the reform process.

Donors are confronted with the simultaneous need to develop new policies for post-conflict environments and to implement peacebuilding programs. The force of events will provide many changes before adequate reflection can take place. Nonetheless, analytic work should continue in order to gain a deeper understanding of the internal dynamics of donor assistance for peacebuilding. To date, analyses of peacebuilding activities have focused primarily on the situation in specific war-torn countries and the contribution of the donors in these individual cases. There has been less analysis of the way in which donor institutions respond to the demands of peacebuilding.

To facilitate the process of determining how practices and policies need to be modified, it would be helpful to have both an internal and an external perspective on donor activities. Thus, donors should examine their own policies and activities. In 1995, for example, the World Bank commissioned internal studies of its operations in countries emerging from prolonged periods of internal conflict and in countries that have disintegrated or are in danger of doing so. In addition, external analysts should conduct case studies of the activities of specific donors in the same way that they have evaluated peacebuilding activities in particular war-torn countries.

In-depth analyses of specific types of peacebuilding activities could be helpful in determining the most cost-effective method of meeting specific objectives. Virtually every donor institution is facing financial constraints, and these are likely to intensify in the near term. It is critical that donors evaluate just what their financial investment buys. Although the situation in each war-torn country dictates a somewhat different approach to any given task—such as reforming the police, reintegrating the most war-affected populations, or strengthening the judicial system—a review of as large a number of individual programs as possible will indicate necessary program components, optional program components, relative financial and political costs of different approaches, and so on. This approach has been applied to the demobilization and reintegration of former combatants and is now beginning to generate specific suggestions for program design and implementation strategies.

■　■　■

Post-conflict reconstruction has now captured the attention of the international development community. As this essay demonstrates, there is sufficient accumulated experience from past peacebuilding efforts to identify the broad outlines of a donor strategy for post-conflict reconstruction and reconciliation. The next step is to agree on priority areas and translate this experience into operational guidelines for each of those areas. At the same time, the international community should not lose sight of the fact that the responsibility for moving from war to peace is ultimately the responsibility of the people and the governments of war-torn countries. Donor strategies need, therefore, to give particular emphasis to creating an environment in which reconstruction and reconciliation can take root and to building capacity in both the public and the private sectors. Only then will war-torn countries be able to take advantage of a climate favorable to the consolidation of peace.

List of Acronyms

BPD	Banco Popular de Desenvolvimento (Mozambique)
CCF	Cease-Fire Commission (Mozambique)
CCFADM	Joint Commission for the Formation of the Mozambican Defense Force
CG	Consultative Group
CMAC	Cambodian Mine-Action Center
CORE	Reintegration Commission (Mozambique)
CPP	Cambodian People's Party
CSC	Supervisory and Monitoring Commission (Mozambique)
DAC	Development Assistance Committee of the OECD
DHA	United Nations Department of Humanitarian Affairs
FAES	Armed Forces of El Salvador
FADM	Mozambican Defence Force
FMLN	Frente Farabundo Martí para la Liberación Nacional (El Salvador)
FUNCINPEC	United Front for an Independent, Neutral, Peaceful, and Cooperative Cambodia
IMF	International Monetary Fund
NGO	Nongovernmental organization
NRP	National Reconstruction Plan (El Salvador)
OECD	Organisation for Economic Co-operation and Development
ONUMOZ	United Nations Observer Mission in Mozambique

ONUSAL	United Nations Observer Mission in El Salvador
PCN	National Civil Police (El Salvador)
PDC	Christian Democratic Party (El Salvador)
PKO	Peacekeeping operation
PTT	Land Transfer Program (El Salvador)
RCG	Royal Cambodian Government (post-May 1993 elections)
RSS	Reintegration Support Scheme (Mozambique)
SRSG	Special Representative of the United Nations Secretary-General
SOC	State of Cambodia (prior to May 1993 elections)
SRN	National Secretariat for Reconstruction (El Salvador)
UNDP	United Nations Development Programme
UNOHAC	United Nations Office for Humanitarian Assistance Coordination (Mozambique)
UNTAC	United Nations Transitional Authority Cambodia
USAID	United States Agency for International Development

Notes

[1] In 1994, for example, some 10 percent of total official development assistance was absorbed by nonfood emergency programs of all types, a fivefold increase since 1980.

[2] In the words of the Development Assistance Committee Secretariat of the Organisation of Economic Co-operation and Development (OECD) in mid-1994, "The prevailing mode is still one of crisis management."

[3] Paul Collier, "Introduction," in Jean-Paul Azam et al., *Some Economic Consequences of the Transition from Civil War to Peace*, Policy Research Working Paper 1392 (Washington, DC: World Bank, December 1994), pp. 4-5.

[4] See, for example, Elisa Dos Santos, João Honwana, and Miguel de Brito, "The Conflict in Mozambique: Preliminary Report," prepared for the Program on Enhancing Security and Development, Overseas Development Council (Maputo, March 1995), p. 85.

Not all countries emerge from conflict with crushing debt burdens, however. In 1993, the World Bank noted:

> "El Salvador has a relatively low external debt burden with the bulk of external development financing provided by official sources on concessional terms. As a result of the war, little commercial debt was incurred during the 1980s, and the U.S. was the only significant bilateral donor. In December 1992 the U.S. forgave US$463 million, amounting to 75 percent of USAID and P.L. 480 debt, bringing total external debt down from 33 percent of GDP in 1992 to 25 percent in 1993."

See World Bank, "Report and Recommendations of the International Bank for Reconstruction and Development to the Executive Directors on a Proposed Second Structural Adjustment Loan (SAL) of US$50 Million to the Republic of El Salvador" (Washington, DC: World Bank, August 23, 1993), pp. 20-21.

In addition, 90 percent of the $1.1 billion in military assistance provided by the United States between 1979 and 1991 was in the form of grants, and military purchases from the United States accounted for an estimated 4 percent of El Salvador's total debt in 1991. *U.S. Overseas Loans and Grants and Assistance from International Organizations* (1982, 1986, 1989, and 1992), pp. 47, 49, 49, and 97, respectively; U.S. Department of State and U.S. Department of Defense, Defense Security Assistance Agency, *Congressional Presentation for Security Assistance Programs, Fiscal Year 1994* (Washington, DC), p. 178.

[5] Moreover, for three of the countries that form the core of this study, the demise of the Soviet bloc eliminated major trading partners as well as sources of aid.

[6] This shortage is often heightened artificially by the international community. In Nicaragua, for example, university-educated professionals can earn more in three days as donor consultants than they would in one month as government employees.

[7] See, for example, U.S. Department of State, *Hidden Killers: The Global Land Mine Crisis*, Publication 10225 (Washington, DC: U.S. Dept. of State, December 1994); Arms Project and Physicians for Human Rights, *Land Mines: A Deadly Legacy* (New York: Human Rights Watch, 1993).

[8] See, for example, Republic of El Salvador, Ministry of Planning and Coordination of Economic and Social Development, *National Reconstruction Plan: Executive Summary* (San Salvador, February 1992), p. 3.

[9] The security establishment consists of the armed forces (army, navy, air force), intelligence forces, police, and paramilitary forces.

[10] Some donors and international organizations face substantial learning curves of their own. Conflicts often limit their access to portions of the territory, and some agencies may withdraw entirely from a country during a conflict. In addition, conflicts sometimes create new countries and almost always transform the societies in which they occur. Some methods of overcoming these problems are discussed in Part IV of this essay.

[11] These phases do not apply to circumstances in which a civil war ends with the victory of one party. However, the problems confronted by the government and society in these countries are very similar to those faced by countries where wars end with negotiated settlements, and many of the lessons outlined in Part IV of this essay are applicable to them as well.

[12] For example, the mid-1993 appointment of a former officer of the El Salvador Armed Forces to head the National Civil Police was an act expressly forbidden by the peace treaty.

[13] See, for example, UNDP, Regional Bureau for Latin America and the Caribbean, *Final Progress Report: Emergency Programme for Persons in Process of Demobilization in El Salvador* (New York: UNDP, February 1993), p. 4.

[14] Sarah Keener, Suzanne Heigh, Luiz Pereira da Silva, and Nicole Ball, *Demobilization and Reintegration of Military Personnel in Africa*, Africa Regional Series, Discussion Paper (Washington, DC: World Bank, 1993), pp. 31–34.

[15] These are the definitions used by the U.S. Office of Foreign Disaster Assistance as reported in Barry Stein, "Returnee Aid and Development," evaluation report submitted to the Central Evaluation Section, U.N. High Commissioner for Refugees (September 29, 1993), unpublished.

[16] Anthony Lake and contributors, *After the Wars: Reconstruction in Afghanistan, Indochina, Central America, Southern Africa, and the Horn of Africa*, U.S.-Third World Policy Perspectives No.16 (New Brunswick, NJ: Transaction Publishers in cooperation with the Overseas Development Council, 1990), pp. 16-17.

[17] For lessons derived from previous demobilization and reintegration efforts, see Nicole Ball, "Demobilization and Reintegration of Soldiers: Findings from Africa," in *Rebuilding War-Torn Societies: Critical Areas for International Assistance*, ed. Krishna Kumar (Boulder, CO: Lynne Rienner, 1996); Nat Colletta, Markus Kostner, and Ingo Wiederhofer, *War to Peace Transition in Sub-Saharan Africa: Lessons from the Horn, the Heart, and the Cape* (Washington, DC: World Bank, 1996); and Keener et al., *Demobilization and Reintegration*, op. cit. Although these three studies have focused primarily on African experiences, most of the lessons are relevant to other regions.

[18] U.S. Department of State, *Hidden Killers: 1994*, op. cit., pp. 35-36. See also, Arms Project and Physicians for Human Rights, *Land Mines*, op. cit.

[19] Development Associates, Inc., *Final Report: Evaluation of the Peace and National Recovery Project, El Salvador* (Arlington, VA: Development Associates, Inc., January 1994), p. IX-1.

[20] USAID, "Providing Humanitarian Assistance and Aiding Post-Crisis Transitions: USAID's Strategy," unpublished, ca. 1994.

[21] "The IMF in Africa: Affray," *The Economist* (October 28, 1995), p. 46.

[22] United Nations, *Declaration on the Rehabilitation and Reconstruction of Cambodia*, document *A/46/608-S/23177* (New York: United Nations, October 30, 1991), para. 2.

[23] Neither USAID nor any other donor is likely to have access to such a substantial amount of counterpart funds with any frequency.

[24] The budget of the Office of Transition Initiatives (OTI) for FY1995 was $20 million; for FY1996, it was $25 million. These sums were never meant to sustain programs; they were meant to serve as a stopgap between the end of a crisis and the arrival of aid from bilateral donors, U.N. agencies, and international financial institutions. USAID Administrator Brian Atwood has recognized that a more significant effort is required, but the political attacks on foreign assistance in the mid-1990s have prevented USAID from raising significantly the budget allocated to OTI.

At the same time, one must ask whether creating a separate office perpetuates the division between "genuine" development and the types of intervention required during the transition phase. Providing this unit with limited authority, staff, and financing increases the risk that it will be perceived as ineffectual and deepens the disinclination to cope with post-conflict transitions that is already evident within the U.S. government.

Opening a special window might, in the long run, be more productive than creating a separate, OTI-type office. World Bank President James Wolfensohn has proposed to the executive directors of the Bank that a fund be established to help jump-start critical post-conflict activities immediately after hostilities cease. This fund would be accessible to all relevant Bank units and would not design or carry out its own projects. In fact, fund resources would be used solely to finance projects and would not cover Bank staff or other Bank resources that would be the responsibility of the Bank's ordinary administrative budget. The fund would be financed from the World Bank surplus. Contributions from other donors would also be sought. Among the activities that might be covered by such a fund are as follows: damage and needs assessments, support to priority mine clearance, rehabilitation of critical economic and social infrastructure, demobilization, social funds, and financial and technical assistance to restart local and national governments.

[25] The Dutch, for example, are delegating broad expenditure authority to embassies and field offices.

[26] UNDP, *Launching New Protagonists in Salvadoran Agriculture* (San Salvador: UNDP, December 1993), p. 72.

[27] Ibid., p. 32.

[28] For example, see "Rebuilding Post-War Rwanda: Evaluating the Impact of International Assistance," report of Team IV, Multi-Donor Evaluation of Emergency Assistance to Rwanda, second draft (Washington, DC: USAID, October 2, 1995), p. 64.

[29] USAID/El Salvador, "The First Three Years of the Peace and National Recovery Project (519-0394): Lessons Learned" (San Salvador: USAID, October 1994), p. 25.

[30] Ibid., pp. 34, 47-52; UNDP, Regional Bureau for Latin America and the Caribbean, op. cit., p. 10, para. 44; Development Associates, Inc., *Evaluation of the Peace and National Recovery Project (519-0394)* (Arlington, VA: DAI, January 1994), pp. III-34-III-35.

[31] USAID/El Salvador, "The First Three Years," op. cit.

[32] Development Associates, Inc., op. cit., pp. V-10/11 and VII-8.

[33] It might be argued as well that parties to the conflict did not represent the interests of many noncombatants *during* the conflict.

[34] U.N. General Assembly/Security Council, *Supplement to an Agenda for Peace: Position Paper of the Secretary-General on the Occasion of the Fiftieth Anniversary of the United Nations* (January 25, 1995), para. 22.

[35] Donors are by no means the sole source of financial and technical assistance. Ministries of finance and private enterprise also have a role to play.

[36] "Statement by Mark L. Schneider, Head of Delegation U.S. Government to the Informal Donors Meeting for Guatemala," Paris, June 21, 1995, p. 7.

[37] "Final Trip Report, USAID/State Mission to Angola, December 12-21, 1994" (Washington, DC: USAID, January 1995), p. 15.

[38] The Calderón Sol government has taken steps that may overcome a number of the obstacles to implementing the land transfer program in El Salvador. See James K. Boyce et al., *Adjustment Toward Peace: Economic Policy and Post-War Reconstruction in El Salvador* (San Salvador: UNDP, May 1995), pp. 56-57.

[39] See, for example, United Nations, S/RES/920, May 26, 1994; and United Nations, S/RES/961, November 23, 1994.

[40] U.N. General Assembly, *Strengthening the Coordination of Humanitarian and Disaster Relief of the United Nations, Including Special Economic Assistance: Special Economic Assistance to Individual Countries or Regions: Assistance for Reconstruction and Development of El Salvador*, document A/50/455 (October 23, 1995), annex II, para. 73.

[41] The Nicaraguan peace process was not governed by a peace agreement negotiated specifically to address the issues dividing the Sandinista government from the Nicaraguan Resistance. Rather, it began as the result of a series of agreements among the leaders of five Central American countries designed to bring peace to the region. One of these agreements, the Tela Accord, of August 7, 1989, called on the Nicaraguan Resistance (the *contras*) to disarm and accept repatriation to Nicaragua or a third country. An earlier accord, Esquipulas II, had called for elections in each of the signatory countries, but none of the agreements required the government forces to be demobilized. Nonetheless, to reduce costs, the Sandinista government began to reduce the size of the Sandinista People's Army in 1989, primarily by releasing reserves and reducing the number of conscripts inducted into the force.

[42] Personal communication from George Vickers, executive director, Washington Office on Latin America, November 20, 1995.

[43] In addition, the parties often exaggerate the number of men and women under arms and are concerned that allowing access to their troops will enable an accurate count to be made.

[44] Privatization should not include the purchase of government assets by active duty military officers or their immediate families.

[45] OECD, "Development Assistance Committee Orientations on Participatory Development and Good Governance," OECD/GD(93)191 (Paris: OECD, 1993), pp. 19-21.

[46] "Chair's Closing Statement," Mozambique Consultative Group Meeting, Paris, March 14-15, 1995.

[47] USAID/El Salvador, "The First Three Years," op. cit.

[48] Development Associates, Inc., op. cit., pp. IV-1–IV-4.

[49] Ibid., pp. IV-2. This comment is supported by a growing consensus among practitioners involved in developing and implementing reintegration programs that, to the extent possible,

programs targeted to demobilized soldiers should be limited in scope and duration and that reintegration should be integrated into post-war rehabilitation and reconstruction efforts aimed at civilians as well as former combatants.

[50] Another consideration is simply that the senior command had no idea what their troops wanted and never thought to ask them; they simply made assumptions based on what the FMLN requested.

[51] On this point, see Patricia Weiss Fagen, "El Salvador: Lessons in Peace Consolidation," in ed., Tom Farer, *Beyond Sovereignty: Collectively Defending Democracy in the Americas* (Baltimore, MD: Johns Hopkins University Press, 1996).

[52] UNDP, *Launching New Protagonists*, op. cit., pp. 25-26.

[53] Weiss Fagen, op. cit. See also United Nations, "Report of the Secretary-General on the Activities of ONUSAL since the Cease-fire (1 February 1992) between the Government of El Salvador and the FMLN," document S/23999 (May 26, 1992), para. 25-26.

[54] Keener et al., *Demobilization and Reintegration*, op. cit., and Colletta, Kostner, and Wieder-hofer, *War-to-Peace Transition*, op. cit.

[55] Unfortunately, in this situation, the United Nations is not the only actor that has learned lessons from the Salvadoran peace process. The Guatemalan military is reportedly determined not to repeat the mistakes of its Salvadoran colleagues who, senior Guatemalan military officials believe, made far too many concessions during the peace negotiations.

[56] Becoming more politically aware is not the same as including political development in an institution's mandate.

[57] Joanna Macrae and Anthony Zwi with Vivienne Forsythe, *Post-Conflict Rehabilitation: Preliminary Issues for Consideration by the Health Sector* (London: Health Policy Unit, London School of Hygiene and Tropical Medicine, 1995), p. 51.

[58] World Bank, "Report and Recommendations," op. cit., p. 18, para. 51.

[59] The process of involving opposition NGOs in National Reconstruction Plan activities has been highly politicized. See, for example, Kevin Murray with Ellen Coletti, Jack Spence, et al., *Rescuing Reconstruction: The Debate on Post-War Economic Recovery in El Salvador* (Cambridge, MA, and San Salvador: Hemisphere Initiatives, May 1994), pp. 16-21, and U.S. Government Accounting Office, *El Salvador: Implementation of Post-War Programs Slower Than Expected* (Washington, DC, January 1994), pp. 13, 22. Although it is clear that the government preferred to exclude opposition NGOs from National Reconstruction Plan activi-ties in order to weaken their potential political impact, it is also clear that these NGOs needed considerable assistance to transform themselves from wartime relief and political organizations to entities capable of providing effective, timely assistance to target populations. As a result of pressure from USAID/Washington and the U.S. Congress, USAID/El Salvador has become more supportive of opposition NGOs.

[60] Development Associates, Inc., op. cit., pp. VII-8–VII-9.

[61] Murray with Coletti, Spence et al., op. cit., p. 19. The need to adopt more participatory styles of governing is a problem that FMLN mayors have also been confronting since the March 1994 elections. See Mario Lungo, "FMLN Mayors in 15 Towns," *NACLA Report on the Americas*, Vol. 29, No. 1 (July-August 1995), pp. 33-36.

[62] Nguyuru H. I. Lipumba, *Africa Beyond Adjustment*, Policy Essay No. 15 (Washington, DC: Overseas Development Council, 1994), p. 85.

[63] See, for example, Stephen Lister and Mike Stevens, "Aid Coordination and Management" (Washington, DC: World Bank Operations Group, April 22, 1992), and OECD, *Development Co-operation: Efforts and Policies of the Members of the Development Assistance Committee, 1988 Report* (Paris, 1988), pp. 109-123.

[64] "Peace Agreement Between the Government of El Salvador and the FMLN" (New York: United Nations, January 16, 1992), chap. V, sec. 9.

[65] See, for example, Lister and Stevens, op. cit., and Robert Cassen et al., *Does Aid Work?* (Oxford: Clarendon Press, 1986), p. 227.

[66] World Bank, *Strengthening the Effectiveness of Aid: Lessons for Donors* (Washington, DC: World Bank, 1995), p. 13, and Lister and Stevens, op. cit., p. 33.

About the Authors

NICOLE BALL is an ODC Fellow, and she directed the Program on Enhancing Security and Development at the Overseas Development Council. She joined ODC in August 1991 to examine the role that economic aid and other financial flows can play in promoting change in the military sectors of developing countries. Since 1994, she has focused on the ways in which development cooperation agencies can assist peacebuilding. Ball has held research positions at the University of Sussex and the Swedish Institute for International Affairs. From 1987 to 1990, she was Director of Analysis at the National Security Archive. She has consulted for the World Bank, the Global Coalition for Africa, the U.N. International Labour Office, the Japan International Cooperation Agency, and the Ministry for Foreign Affairs of Sweden on measuring military expenditure, opportunities for reducing military budgets, defense industry conversion, reintegrating ex-combatants, and rebuilding war-torn countries. Ball has written widely on the relationship between security and development in the developing world. Her publications include *Regional Conflicts and the International System: A Case Study of Bangladesh* (University of Sussex, 1975); *World Hunger: A Guide to the Economic and Political Dimensions* (ABC-Clio, 1982); *The Military in the Development Process* (Regina, 1982); *The Structure of the Defense Industry: An International Survey* (co-edited, Croom-Helm, 1983); *Converting Military Facilities (ILO, 1985); Security and Economy in the Third World* (Princeton, 1988); *Briefing Book on Conventional Arms Transfers* (Council for a Livable World Education Fund, 1991); *Pressing for Peace: Can Aid Induce Reform?* (ODC, 1992); and *Demobilization and Reintegration of Military Personnel in Africa: The Evidence from Seven Country Case Studies* (with Sarah Keener, Suzanne Heigh, and Luiz Pereira da Silva, World Bank, 1993).

TAMMY HALEVY served as the Assistant Director of ODC's Program on Enhancing Security and Development. Before joining ODC, she was a research assistant for Harvard Law School's Program on International Financial Systems and an instructor in Slovakia under the auspices of Education for Democracy.

About the ODC

ODC is an international policy research institute based in Washington, D.C., that seeks to inform and improve the multilateral approaches and institutions—both global and regional—that will play increasingly important roles in the promotion of development and the management of related global problems.

ODC's program of multilateral analysis and dialogue is designed to explore ideas and approaches for enhancing global cooperation, to build networks of new leadership among public and private actors around the world, and to inform decisionmaking on selected development topics of broad international concern.

ODC is private, nonprofit organization funded by foundations, corporations, governments, and private individuals. Funding for the U.S. Program comes exclusively from U.S. foundations, corporations, and individuals.

Stephen J. Friedman is the Chairman of the Overseas Development Council, and the Council's President is John W. Sewell.

Board of Directors